CRE▲TIVE
HOMEOWNER®

SMART GUIDE

ponds & fountains
step-by-step projects

CREATIVE HOMEOWNER®, Upper Saddle River, New Jersey

Editorial Director: Timothy O. Bakke
Production Manager: Kimberly H. Vivas
Art Director: Annie Jeon

Author: Jim Barrett
Editors: Laura Tringali, David Schiff, Fran J. Donegan
Editorial Assistant: Jennifer Ramcke
Photo Researcher: Sharon Ranftle
Copyeditor: Marilyn Gilbert
Technical Consultants: Wayne Arter, Cal Pump; John Hetzel, Henri Studio Inc.;
    James A. Lawrie, Waterford Gardens; Paul Martin, Beckett Corp.; Lynn Nissom,
    Lilies of the Valley Water Gardens; Charles B. Thomas and Virginia Crumb,
    Lilypons Water Gardens; William C. Uber, Van Ness Water Gardens

Senior Designer: David Geer
Illustrator: Norman Nuding
Cover: Gary G. Wittstock/Pond Supplies of America (photography),
    Clarke Barre (design)

Current Printing (last digit)
10 9 8 7 6 5 4

Smart Guide: Ponds & Fountains
Library of Congress Control Number: 2002104993
ISBN: 1-58011-106-8

CREATIVE HOMEOWNER®
A Division of Federal Marketing Corp.
24 Park Way
Upper Saddle River, NJ 07458

Metric Conversion

Length

1 inch	25.4 mm
1 foot	0.3048 m
1 yard	0.9144 m
1 mile	1.61 km

Area

1 square inch	645 mm²
1 square foot	0.0929 m²
1 square yard	0.8361 m²
1 acre	4046.86 m²
1 square mile	2.59 km²

Volume

1 cubic inch	16.3870 cm³
1 cubic foot	0.03 m³
1 cubic yard	0.77 m³

Common Lumber Equivalents

Sizes: Metric cross sections are so close to their U.S. sizes, as noted below, that for most purposes they may be considered equivalents.

Dimensional lumber		
	1 × 2	19 × 38 mm
	1 × 4	19 × 89 mm
	2 × 2	38 × 38 mm
	2 × 4	38 × 89 mm
	2 × 6	38 × 140 mm
	2 × 8	38 × 184 mm
	2 × 10	38 × 235 mm
	2 × 12	38 × 286 mm

Capacity

1 fluid ounce	29.57 mL
1 pint	473.18 mL
1 quart	1.14 L
1 gallon	3.79 L

Weight

1 ounce	28.35g
1 pound	0.45kg

Temperature

Fahrenheit = Celsius × 1.8 + 32
Celsius = Fahrenheit − 32 × 5/9

Nail Size & Length

Penny Size	Nail Length
2d	1"
3d	1¼"
4d	1½"
5d	1¾"
6d	2"
7d	2¼"
8d	2½"
9d	2¾"
10d	3"
12d	3¼"

Photo Credits

page 1: Gary G. Wittstock/Pond Supplies of America, Inc., Yorkville, IL, 630-553-0033 **page 3:** *top* Jacqueline Murphy/CH; *top middle and center* Gary G. Wittstock/Pond Supplies of America, Inc.; *bottom* J. Paul Moore **page 5:** *top left* Jennifer Ramcke, courtesy of Alex Bartusiavicius; *top right* Robert Perron; *bottom right* Jacqueline Murphy/CH; *bottom left* Brian Nieves/CH, courtesy of Waterford Gardens; *middle left* Jacqueline Murphy/CH **page 17:** *top left, top middle, and top right* Gary G. Woodstock/Pond Supplies of America, Inc.; *bottom right* Saxon Holt; *bottom left* Edifice Photo/Gillian Darley **page 23:** *top left and top right* Gary G. Wittstock/Pond Supplies of America, Inc.; *bottom right* Joan Lebold Cohen/Photo Researchers; *bottom left* judywhite/New Leaf Images **page 33:** *top left* Saxon Holt; *top right* John Glover, designer: Pamela Woods; *bottom right* Roger Foley; *bottom left* Ken Druse **page 37:** *top left* Gary G. Wittstock/Pond Supplies of America, Inc.; *top right* Jennifer Ramcke, courtesy of Jerry Savitske; *bottom right* Jennifer Ramcke, courtesy of Alex

Bartusiavicius; *bottom left* Ron Sutherland/Garden Picture Library **page 51:** *top left* courtesy of Charleston Gardens; *top middle* John Glover; *top right and bottom right* Jacqueline Murphy/CH; *bottom left* Jennifer Ramcke, courtesy of Bar Harbor Township **page 57:** *top left* Brad Simmons, architect: Greg Staley; *top right* Pam Spaulding/Positive Images; *bottom* Brian Nieves/CH, courtesy of Waterford Gardens **page 61:** *top left, top middle, and top right* Gary G. Wittstock/Pond Supplies of America, Inc.; *bottom* Ron Sutherland/Garden Picture Library **page 67:** *top left* Jacqueline Murphy/CH; *top right* courtesy of Van Ness Water Gardens; *right center* Jack Jennings/Missouri Botanical Gardens; *bottom right* Gary G. Wittstock/Pond Supplies of America, Inc.; *bottom left* Jennifer Ramcke, courtesy of Jerry Savitske; *center* Jack Jennings/Missouri Botanical Gardens; *left center* Missouri Botanical Gardens **page 73:** *top* Ken Druse; *bottom right and bottom left* Gary G. Wittstock/Pond Supplies of America, Inc.

contents

Chapter 1 Planning 5
• Selecting a Sight • Pond Styles • Lighting • Making a Site Plan

Chapter 2 Pond Options 17
• Flexible Pond Liners • Premolded Pond Shells • Concrete Ponds • Other Options • Pond Depth & Capacity

Chapter 3 Flexible Liners 23
• Sizing the Liner • Installing the Liner

Chapter 4 Rigid Liners 33
• Basic Requirements • Shell Installation

Chapter 5 Falls & Streams 37
• Planning Pointers • Sizing the Waterfall • Choosing a Pump • Waterfall Types • Streams • Lining the Watercourse • Installing a Preformed Watercourse • Installing a Lined Watercourse • Installing the Pump

Chapter 6 Fountains 51
• Types of Fountains • Installing a Fountain Spray • Installing a Statuary Fountain • Installing the Fountain

Chapter 7 Bridges 57
• Wooden Bridges • Stepping-stones

Chapter 8 Healthy Water 61
• Balancing the Water • Filtration

Chapter 9 Pond Life 67
• Aquatic Plants • Fish & Other Water Creatures

Chapter 10 Maintenance 73
• Pond Care • Repairing a Pond Liner

Glossary 79

Index 80

safety first

Though all the designs and methods in this book have been reviewed for safety, it is not possible to overstate the importance of using the safest construction methods possible. What follows are reminders; some do's and don'ts of basic carpentry. They are not substitutes for your own common sense.

- *Always* use caution, care, and good judgment when following the procedures described in this book.

- *Always* be sure that the electrical setup is safe; be sure that no circuit is overloaded and that all power tools and electrical outlets are properly grounded. Do not use power tools in wet locations.

- *Always* read container labels on paints, solvents, and other products; provide ventilation, and observe all other warnings.

- *Always* read the manufacturer's instructions for using a tool, especially the warnings.

- *Always* use hold-downs and push sticks whenever possible when working on a table saw. Avoid working short pieces if you can.

- *Always* remove the key from any drill chuck (portable or press) before starting the drill.

- *Always* pay deliberate attention to how a tool works so that you can avoid being injured.

- *Always* know the limitations of your tools. Do not try to force them to do what they were not designed to do.

- *Always* make sure that any adjustment is locked before proceeding. For example, always check the rip fence on a table saw or the bevel adjustment on a portable saw before starting to work.

- *Always* clamp small pieces firmly to a bench or other work surface when using a power tool on them.

- *Always* wear the appropriate rubber or work gloves when handling chemicals, moving or stacking lumber, or doing heavy construction.

- *Always* wear a disposable face mask when you create dust by sawing or sanding. Use a special filtering respirator when working with toxic substances and solvents.

- *Always* wear eye protection, especially when using power tools or striking metal on metal or concrete; a chip can fly off, for example, when chiseling concrete.

- *Always* be aware that there is seldom enough time for your body's reflexes to save you from injury from a power tool in a dangerous situation; everything happens too fast. Be alert!

- *Always* keep your hands away from the business ends of blades, cutters, and bits.

- *Always* hold a circular saw firmly, usually with both hands so that you know where they are.

- *Always* use a drill with an auxiliary handle to control the torque when large-size bits are used.

- *Always* check your local building codes when planning new construction. The codes are intended to protect public safety and should be observed to the letter.

- *Never* work with power tools when you are tired or under the influence of alcohol or drugs.

- *Never* cut tiny pieces of wood or pipe using a power saw. Cut small pieces off larger pieces.

- *Never* change a saw blade or a drill or router bit unless the power cord is unplugged. Do not depend on the switch being off; you might accidentally hit it.

- *Never* work in insufficient lighting.

- *Never* work while wearing loose clothing, hanging hair, open cuffs, or jewelry.

- *Never* work with dull tools. Have them sharpened, or learn how to sharpen them yourself.

- *Never* use a power tool on a workpiece—large or small—that is not firmly supported.

- *Never* saw a workpiece that spans a large distance between horses without close support on each side of the cut; the piece can bend, closing on and jamming the blade, causing saw kickback.

- *Never* support a workpiece from underneath with your leg or other part of your body when sawing.

- *Never* carry sharp or pointed tools, such as utility knives, awls, or chisels, in your pocket. If you want to carry such tools, use a special-purpose tool belt with leather pockets and holders.

planning

Selecting a Site

Even if you've already chosen what you think is the perfect spot for your pond, consider one or two alternate sites. Before making a final decision, think about the following points: What is the purpose of the pond? Should it dress up a bleak corner of the yard, provide a quiet place for meditation, or complement a deck, patio, or other existing feature? How accessible should the pond be? Do you want to stroll to it over a rambling path, or simply step out to it through your back door? Should the pond be secluded, or visible from inside the house so that you can enjoy it year-round? How will the sun, shade, and wind patterns of your property affect the placement of the pond? How easy will it be to provide water and electricity to the pond site? Will the excavation interfere with existing underground pipes and cables?

Proximity to the House. A pond visible from the house——perhaps through a large picture window or sliding glass doors——will provide pleasure, even in cold or inclement weather. Add underwater or low garden lighting around the pond perimeter, and you'll create a dramatic evening view. By contrast, a pond isolated from the house, perhaps surrounded by tall shrubs or screens, can become a private retreat, a peaceful place where family members can escape from day-to-day routines. A pond or fountain near the front entrance of the house adds an attractive focal point to the landscape. It also gives visitors something to admire while waiting outside your door. If your property is large enough, you can tuck a small pond in a side yard, perhaps to be viewed from a kitchen or bedroom window. If your yard is very small, you may simply wish to locate the pond right in its center, and then work all other landscape features (such as walks, plantings, and seating) around it.

Sun, Shade, and Wind. The pond site will require plenty of sunlight if you plan to grow flowering water plants. During the summer months, water lilies, for example, require at

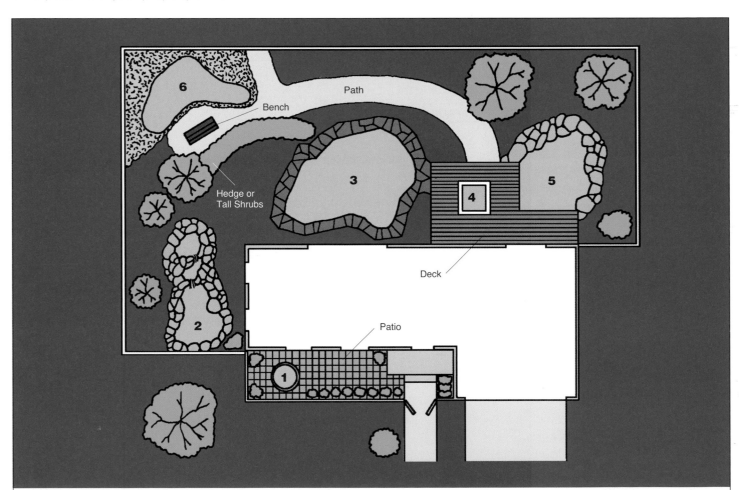

Selecting a Site. When selecting a site for your pond, decide how close you want it to the house and from which room or rooms you want to view it. A small formal pond or fountain **(1)** greets visitors at the front entry. A series of small ponds connected by short waterfalls **(2)** fits neatly into a narrow side yard. A large pond **(3)** is a dramatic focal point when viewed from a picture window. A pond incorporated into an attached deck or patio **(4),** or adjacent to it **(5),** can be easily viewed indoors or out. A pond in a far corner of the yard, away from the house **(6),** becomes a secluded retreat.

least six to eight hours of daily direct sunlight to bloom, although some varieties will bloom with as few as three or four hours of direct sun. The more direct sunlight the pond receives each day, the more choices of water plants you will have.

If you'll be adding fish to the pond, you'll have to balance the sun with some shade during the hottest part of the day. Shade can be provided from water lily or lotus pads, tall plants or shrubs around the pond border, a nearby fence or other structure, or a portable shade screen. You can make a simple, lightweight shade screen by building a wooden frame and covering it with a light-colored canvas, landscape fabric, or similar material. You can then position it to shade the pond during the hottest part of the day. Small ponds or tub gardens (100 gallons or less) also profit from some shade, since high water temperatures can promote excessive algae growth and increase water evaporation.

Even though some shade is desirable, you should avoid siting your pond under or next to large trees, because the falling leaves or needles will foul the water and accumulate on the bottom of the pond, clogging the pump/ filtration system. (If there is no other alternative, you can place netting or screen mounted on a wood frame over the pond to catch the leaves during the fall season.) You should also avoid proximity to "messy" trees that could drop excessive blossoms, fruit, or seed pods into the water.

Strong winds can wreak havoc on your pond by blowing leaves, dirt, and other debris into the water. These can increase water evaporation and ruin the effect of a fountain's delicate spray pattern. So, try to site your pond in an area sheltered from strong winds—for example, next to a tall fence or garden wall, the house, or other structure. If these sites don't fit into your plans, you can plant tall, fast-growing evergreen trees or shrubs on the upwind side of the

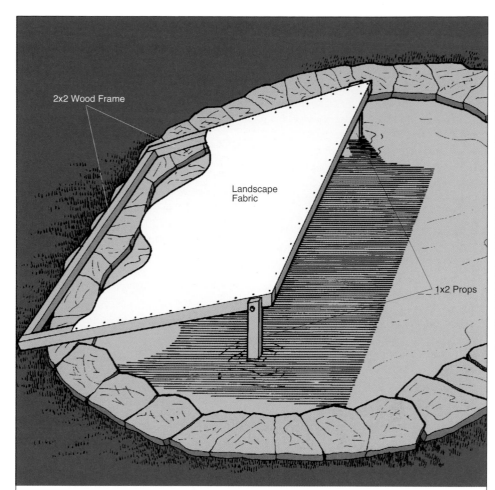

2x2 Wood Frame

Landscape Fabric

1x2 Props

Sun, Shade and Wind. Make a portable shade screen by covering a wooden frame with landscape fabric or canvas.

pond to serve as a windbreak. Tall, dense evergreens, such as spruces and pines, make good windbreaks. Norway spruce and Australian pine are two good choices. So are tall, broad-leafed evergreen trees and tall shrubs, such as eucalyptus, holly, and oleander. If you live in a coastal environment, salt-tolerant species, such as Monterey cypress, Japanese black pine, and Atlas cedar, not only create a windbreak, but they also protect the pond from salt spray.

Trees and tall shrubs generally provide a better windbreak than solid walls or fences because they break the force of the wind over a greater area behind them (typically, for a distance equal to ten times the height of the tree). Wind tends to "wash over" solid barriers and continue at full force several feet behind them.

And don't forget that you should avoid placing the trees too close to the pond, or you'll have problems with falling leaves or needles. You can also erect freestanding lattice screens, perhaps covered with vines, to serve as a windbreak (as well as an attractive backdrop) on the windward side of the pond.

If you've lived in your house for more than a year or two, you probably have a good idea how sun, shade, and wind affect various spots in your yard at different times of the day and in different seasons. In the Northern Hemisphere, a southern exposure (shade screen on the north side of the pond) provides the greatest amount of sunlight year-round, with some late afternoon shade during the summer months. Conversely, a northern exposure (shade screen on the south side of the pond) provides the least amount of sunlight, with some late afternoon sun during the summer. An eastern exposure (shade screen on the west side of the pond) provides morning sun and afternoon shade. So, placing a shade screen on the northwest side of the pond will provide some shade to protect fish during the hottest summer afternoons, while allowing maximum solar gain to help keep water warmer during winter months in mild climates. If you're not sure how sun and shade affect your pond, erect a temporary shade screen, as described on page 7. Experiment with the location for a season or two before installing a permanent shade structure or plantings.

Existing Landscape Features

Determine which existing landscape features in your yard will complement the pond and which will detract from it. For example, siting the pond in one area of the yard may mean that you would have to remove (or prune) one or more large trees or shrubs to provide enough sunlight and to prevent excess leaves from polluting the water. You may have to reroute garden walkways or paths to provide better access to the pond.

View the pond site from several angles to see how it will be visually affected by what lies beyond it. If you've chosen an otherwise perfect location, you may find some eyesores that will need to be removed or disguised. Some unsightly elements, like an old board fence, a metal garden shed, or a bare house wall, can often be masked with plantings.

On the other hand, a pond stuck in the middle of a vast expanse of lawn may look artificial and barren. In this case, plan on how you can dress up the area surrounding the pond—perhaps by adding a rock garden or borders with flowering plants, or maybe a pond-side seating area with benches. Larger shrubs and trees can serve as a pleasant backdrop, either to add dimension to the pond or to screen

unwanted views, like property fences or a neighbor's house. Walks, bridges, ornamental statuary, and similar architectural elements can also be used to add interest to the site.

Remember that the pond must be in scale with the plantings and the architectural features of your property. Don't stuff a large pond into a small side yard. But also remember that a small pond would seem lost adjacent to a voluminous deck.

Soil and Topography

Flat Areas. The best location for a pond is on flat, level, well-drained ground. Even on flat ground, though, the material edging the perimeter of the pond should project at least 2 inches above the surrounding soil to prevent dirt, garden chemicals, and organic matter from polluting the water. In poorly drained clay soils (subject to large puddles of standing water after a heavy rain), grade the

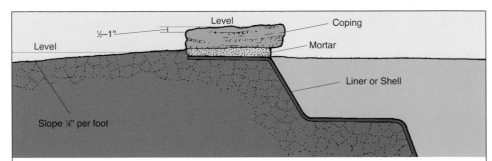

Flat Areas. Ponds are easiest to install on level ground. For good drainage, slope the soil away from pond at least 10 feet in all directions. Edging keeps soil and garden chemicals from washing into the pond.

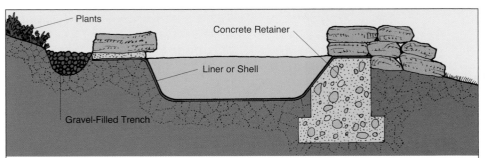

Hillsides. On a hillside, channel the water runoff with a gravel-filled trench on the uphill side of the pond. Ground covers and other plantings help control erosion. Poured concrete or a masonry block retainer supports a pond shell or liner on the downhill side.

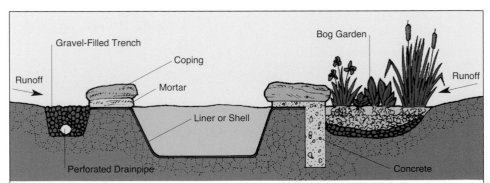

Low-Lying Areas. Avoid low-lying areas for pond sites. If you have no other choice, install a gravel-filled trench with a perforated drainpipe around the pond perimeter to direct surface runoff and subsurface water away from the site. Pipe leads to a dry well at the lower part of the property.

site so the ground slopes away from the pond edges at least 10 feet in all directions. A slope of ⅛-inch per foot will provide good drainage.

Hillsides. Hillside lots are a good opportunity to create beautiful ponds with one or more cascading water-falls, especially if existing rock outcroppings or large boulders can be incorporated. However, hillside sites often present a greater challenge to the builder. Sometimes, extensive grading is required to provide a level area for the pond basin, and to direct runoff from uphill planting areas around the pond. A raised edging will help keep water from washing into the pond. A shallow, gravel-filled trench on the uphill side of the pond may be required to divert heavy runoff.

Low-Lying Areas. A pond usually looks most natural in a low-lying area; but if you place it there, you increase the chance of water runoff entering the pond from all sides. To direct runoff away from the pond edges, you'll need to raise the stone coping 3 to 6 inches above the surrounding soil. Around the perimeter of the pond, you could also install a gravel-filled trench leading to a dry well in a lower part of the yard. Or you can surround the pond with a bog garden. Above-ground ponds also work well in low-lying areas.

Utility Access

You'll need to run electricity to the site if your waterscape will include a pump and/or underwater or perimeter lighting. Some pumps simply plug into a three-prong electrical outlet; others must be "hard-wired" directly into the circuit and controlled by a switch. In either case, you should wire a switch into the circuit so that you can control the pump and lights from inside the house. (For plug-in devices, a switch controls the outlet.)

To get electricity to the pond, you'll need to run an underground electrical cable between the house and

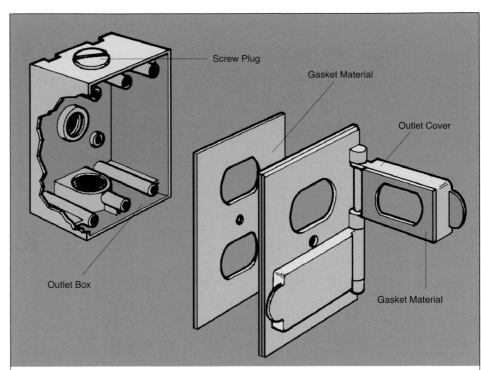

Utility Access. Outdoor electrical boxes are made of thick metal and are fitted with gaskets to protect wiring from the weather.

pond site to provide a convenient outlet in which to plug in the pump. This usually consists of nonmetallic shielded cable (Romex), run inside ½-inch (grey) PVC electrical conduit. But check local electrical codes. Although you may be able to tap into an existing circuit in the house, it is usually best to put the pump and pond lights on a separate circuit, with their own breaker at the main service panel. If you do tap into an existing branch circuit, make sure it has sufficient capacity to handle the additional load of the pump and any outdoor lighting you choose to install. Exterior electrical boxes, shielded cable, and PVC conduit are available at local hardware stores. If the pump and/or lights will be submerged, you probably will need to install a ground fault circuit interrupter (GFCI) or outlet in the electrical circuit. Again, check local codes.

Because ponds and fountains recirculate water, you needn't run a water line directly into the pond or fountain. Just make sure there is a nearby outdoor faucet so you can add water to the pond from a garden

hose as necessary. Small ponds, particularly, may require topping off every week or so during the hottest months of the year. To eliminate this chore, you can run ¼-inch plastic tubing from a nearby water-supply line to the pond, then connect the tubing to a bobby-float valve to maintain a constant water level. (See the drawing, page 50.) These inexpensive setups are available through water-gardening catalog suppliers and nurseries that carry water-garden accessories. Simple ballcock valves, such as those used in toilet tanks, will also work, although these are larger than bobby floats and therefore harder to disguise.

Plan the most direct route possible between the house and pond for utility lines. However, avoid placing lines underneath cement patios, wood decks, or other permanent structures, because they will be harder to access should future repairs be necessary. Also, when siting the pond, make sure the site is not directly over any existing underground pipes, cables, sewer lines, or septic fields.

Pond Styles

The style of your pond is a matter of personal taste, although it will be more attractive if it complements the style of your house, garden, and other existing landscape features like decks and patios. For example, a naturalistic freeform pond with large, moss-covered boulders would look totally out of place in a formal garden with neatly pruned hedges and geometrically shaped planting beds. Conversely, a formal, geometric pond with an ornate fountain spray or classical Greek statue would probably look silly in a natural or informal garden behind a rustic home.

Ponds are generally classified as either informal (those that imitate nature) or formal (those that reflect a particular architectural style). However, this doesn't necessarily mean that you cannot mix natural and architectural elements to come up with a pleasing design. Japanese gardens are a good example of how informal and formal elements can be combined to reflect nature, yet give the viewer a sense of refinement and order.

Formal Ponds

Whether or not a pond is considered formal or informal depends largely on its shape and the edging materials used to define and cover the pond perimeter. Formal ponds and fountains generally conform to strict geometric shapes—circles, ovals, squares, rectangles, octagons, or hexagons. Many formal ponds are raised above the ground and contained by a low wall of concrete, brick, cut stone, or stucco. Often, they include a formal statuary fountain. Such ponds are intended to

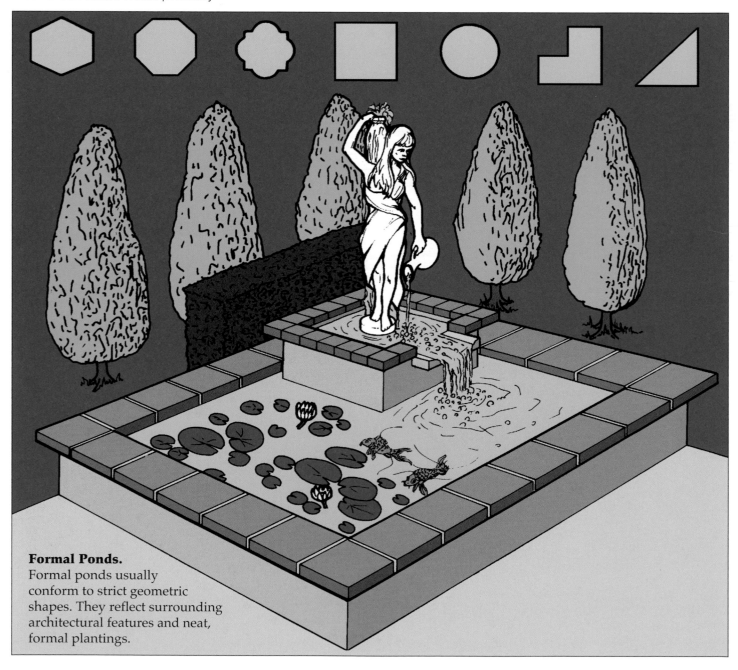

Formal Ponds.
Formal ponds usually conform to strict geometric shapes. They reflect surrounding architectural features and neat, formal plantings.

look man-made and to complement the symmetry of the surrounding garden style and such architectural features on the property as a rectangular deck, a curving patio, or terraced planting areas. If your garden style is formal, with neatly shaped shrubs and hedges and symmetrical planting borders and walks, the pond should follow suit.

The site may also dictate the style. For example, a formal pond may be an extension of another architectural feature, such as a flagstone patio or raised-brick planting bed, or even a masonry wall. If, on the other hand, the pond is located some distance from the house or other structures, it could be formal or informal, as long as the immediately surrounding plantings follow suit. Sunken formal ponds—also geometrical in shape—are often incorporated into patios, decks, masonry walks or formal planting borders. The material used for the surrounding patio, deck or walk features can also be used for the pond edging.

Informal Ponds

Informal ponds take a cue from the pools and streams found in nature. They usually have curvilinear shapes, and often they incorporate a short stream or small waterfall trickling over carefully placed natural rocks. They can also wrap around existing landscape features, such as large boulders or a "peninsula" of tall plantings. Overhanging rocks and perimeter plantings are used to hide the pond edges above the waterline. Informal ponds usually look best in larger yards with informal or natural-looking gardens. But if yard space is limited, a bit of water splashing over a few large rocks into a small reflecting pool can be nearly as effective, suggesting a tiny mountain spring.

Informal or natural ponds must be designed carefully to blend into the surrounding landscape. Some of the most realistic-looking natural ponds incorporate locally quarried stones and native plants. Ferns and moss-covered granite boulders, for

Informal Ponds. Informal ponds simulate nature; they look best in a "wild" setting.

example, would be appropriate in a heavily wooded area, whereas clean, light-colored sandstone rocks with pockets of succulents, reeds, and clumps of bunch grass could suggest an oasis in a desert setting. To complete the natural effect, you can grow water lilies, water iris, lotus, and various bog plants in the pond itself. You should also plan access walks, pond-side sitting areas, and other nearby architectural features carefully, so as not to detract from the natural appearance of the pond.

Bog Gardens

Many ponds and water gardens incorporate marginal plants. (See page 69.) These plants require 2 or 3 inches of water over their roots at all times. Popular marginal plants include water iris, ornamental cattails, horsetail, parrot's feather, and various rush species. You can grow marginal plants in shallow areas of the pond by sinking earth-filled containers below the water surface. Or you can create a separate bog garden or pockets of boggy soil by digging holes or trenches next to the pond, lining them with an EPDM pond liner and filling them with wet soil.

Pond-side bog gardens are separated from the pond by a barrier of compacted soil, mortared stones, or concrete between the bog area and the pond. They are fed by runoff from surrounding garden areas or by direct watering. The barrier prevents soil and garden chemicals from migrating into the pond water and polluting it. Although separate bog gardens are preferable when you want clear, clean pond water, you will need to monitor the soil more frequently so that it doesn't dry out.

In-pond bog gardens have permeable barriers of stacked edging materials, which allow water from the pond to seep into the bog area and keep it constantly moist. A layer of permeable landscape fabric can be used in the barrier to keep excess soil from washing into the pond. Nutrients from the soil will migrate into the pond water, so the soil itself becomes part of the pond ecology. Because the soil nutrients also promote algae growth, the pond may take on a cloudy appearance, especially if it is small. So, if you want an in-pond bog garden, you must plan it so that runoff and chemicals from the surrounding garden don't enter the bog area.

Surrounds and Paths

The style of the walkways and paths around your waterscape should match the style of your pond. For informal ponds, create paths of loose aggregates such as gravel or bark chips; or place large, irregular stepping stones around the pond edge to provide access. If the pond is large enough, you might want to extend the stepping stones into or across the pond itself, or perhaps incorporate a wooden bridge. (See page 58.) Formal ponds may incorporate walks of brick, patio tiles, wood blocks, concrete, cut stone, or similar paving materials. You can extend the path around the perimeter of the pond to encourage strollers to view the pond from different vantage points.

Pond-side seating areas can be as simple as a wooden garden bench placed in a clearing, or as elaborate as a wood deck or masonry patio replete with lawn furniture. Such features should be in scale with the size of the pond and located to provide the best vantage point for viewing it. Don't let surrounding features overwhelm the pond itself.

Edgings

Pond edgings are typically wood or masonry materials that visually define the pond perimeter and keep surrounding soil from washing into the pond. Formal ponds may employ edgings of poured concrete, brick, concrete pavers, patio tiles, wood, or cut stone. Informal ponds generally have natural stone edgings. The edging material you choose should blend into or complement the sur-

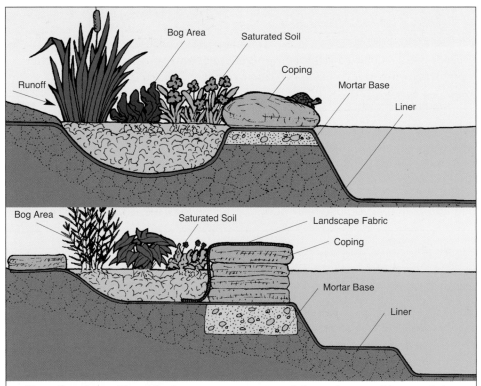

Bog Gardens. Top: The bog area is separated from the pond by a solid barrier of soil, concrete, or coping materials; water collects in the bog area from garden runoff. Bottom: The in-pond bog area is separated by stacked stones or other coping to keep soil in place; water from the pond seeps through the coping to keep bogs moist.

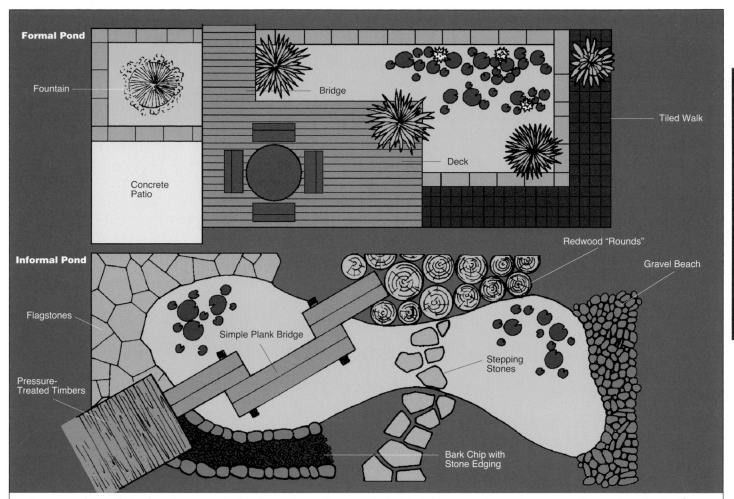

Formal Pond

Fountain

Bridge

Tiled Walk

Concrete Patio

Deck

Redwood "Rounds"

Gravel Beach

Informal Pond

Flagstones

Simple Plank Bridge

Stepping Stones

Pressure-Treated Timbers

Bark Chip with Stone Edging

Surrounds and Paths. Surrounds for formal ponds include brick, tile, concrete, cut stone, and wooden decks that complement the geometric shape of the pond. Informal ponds use more rustic or natural-looking materials: boulders, gravel, cleft flagstones, and the like. Straight lines and sharp edges are softened by plantings.

roundings. Allowing the edging to overhang the pond by a few inches will hide the pond structure.

At least one section of the edging should be wide and flat enough to allow easy access to the pond for maintenance purposes. An over-hanging wooden deck, masonry patio, or flagstone walk bordering the pond could also serve this purpose. Although not absolutely necessary, it is best to mortar the edging stones or masonry units in place, to keep them from being dislodged and slipping into the pond. When installing edging materials, raise them slightly above the surrounding ground to direct runoff away from the pond, as shown.

If you use wood as a edging material, make sure it is pressure-treated with a nontoxic preservative and does not

come in direct contact with the pond water. Most pressure-treated wood sold at lumberyards is suitable; avoid woods treated with pentachlorophe-nol or creosote, which are toxic to fish and plants. If you use redwood,

allow it to season for at least a year (or until it turns grey), since fresh-cut redwood contains toxic tannins. Runoff from an overhanging redwood deck, for example, could leach these toxins from the wood into the pond.

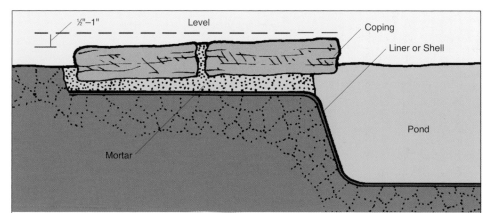

½"–1"   Level

Coping

Liner or Shell

Mortar

Pond

Edgings. Raise the pond edging slightly above the ground to prevent runoff from entering the pond. Slope edging stones away from water.

Lighting

There are several ways to illuminate a pond for night viewing. Underwater lights may immediately come to mind. But they are generally not as effective as a few well-positioned garden lights around the pond perimeter. In order for underwater lights to be effective, the pond water must be fairly clear and the lights positioned to avoid excessive glare. Also, when you place lights underwater, the pond surface loses its reflective quality, which can also be dramatic at night. However, when placed effectively, underwater lights can highlight specimen water lilies, waterfalls, and other features. Some fountain systems, in fact, come equipped with integral underwater lights.

You can also achieve a pleasing effect by directing hidden ground-level spotlights upward to illuminate surrounding trees or tall shrubs and reflect them on the pond surface. Similarly, placing lights at the pond edge to illuminate waterfalls or fountains will create a sparkling effect. Generally, a few well-placed spotlights or accent lights used to highlight specific areas or features in the garden will produce a more desirable effect than strong flood-lights that light up the entire yard.

Also consider using lighting for safety reasons, such as to illuminate walkways or steps leading to the pond. Low-level, ornamental down-lighting fixtures placed at intervals along the borders of a walk, or attached to step railings, provide enough illumination to define the walkways without lighting up the surrounding area.

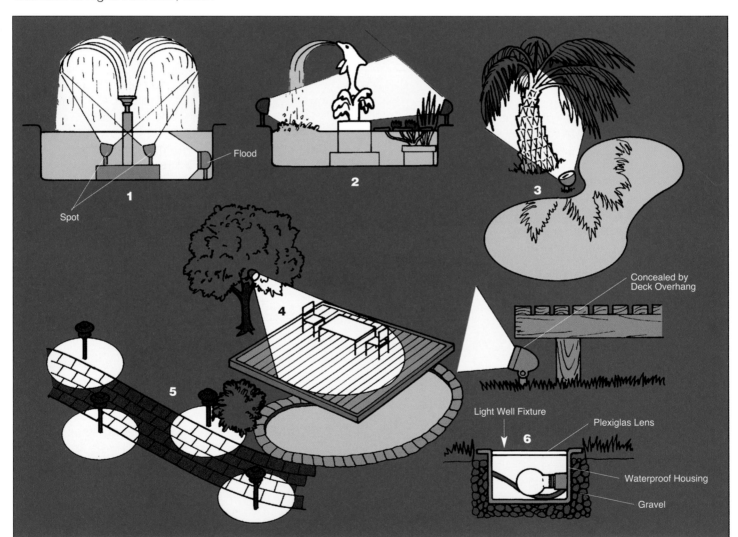

Lighting. 1. Submerged lights can illuminate the entire pond, defining the waterline, or be directed upward at a fountain. **2.** Spotlights at pond edges can be focused on specific areas or features in the pond, such as a specimen water lily or statuary fountain. **3.** Uplighting trees, large shrubs, or other features near the pond can create dramatic reflections on the pond surface. **4.** An overhead floodlight provides general illumination for a pond-side deck or patio; light should be pointed away from pond to avoid glare. **5.** Paths leading to and surrounding the pond should be lighted for safety: Low-intensity downlights at knee level define a path without illuminating the surrounding area. **6.** When possible, conceal fixtures from view.

Fixture Types

A variety of outdoor lighting fixtures is available for producing different effects. You can choose from two basic systems: standard 120-volt systems and low-voltage (12-volt) systems. Standard voltage systems run directly on household current; 12-volt systems require a transformer, which is connected to a 120-volt power source. In general, 12-volt systems are much safer and easier to install than standard systems, and the fixtures and bulbs are much less expensive (most use standard automotive-type bulbs). Many low-voltage systems are available as do-it-yourself kits, but the number of lights and various effects are limited. Bear in mind that low-voltage lights do not produce as much light as standard systems, and so they are not as effective in illuminating large areas. However, they are usually adequate for subtle lighting around ponds. No matter which system you choose, make sure the fixtures, bulbs, connectors, and junction boxes are designed for outdoor use. Because outdoor lighting will be exposed to the weather, the circuit should be protected by a GFCI (ground fault circuit interrupter). You should also check local codes for additional requirements.

Bulbs for outdoor lighting vary in color and intensity. For standard and low-voltage systems, standard tungsten bulbs are the cheapest and most readily available in a variety of wattages. The type most commonly used for outdoor lighting have thickened lenses and built-in reflectors (called PAR bulbs). They come in the form of spotlights, narrow floodlights, and broad floodlights in both high- and low-voltage versions. The more expensive high-intensity halogen bulbs are becoming popular for outdoor lighting, because they produce more light per watt than tungsten bulbs and have a longer life span. The incandescent light produced is a bright, clear white, yet still natural-looking.

Other high-intensity bulbs include mercury vapor (bluish-white), sodium (amber yellow), and metal halide (intense, harsh white). In general, these bulbs are not suitable for the subtle, natural lighting used around ponds, although they're clearly superior to tungsten bulbs for lighting up the whole backyard. Special bulbs and watertight housings are required for underwater lighting. Colored lenses are also available for underwater lights, as well as for general garden lighting, to create a fairyland effect. When planning to use colored lenses to highlight plants and trees, though, you should choose them carefully to avoid giving the foliage an unnatural appearance.

Fixture Placement

Place lighting fixtures to avoid excessive glare off the water surface. Also try to avoid placing lights where they will shine directly into the eyes of the viewer. Because many outdoor light fixtures are utilitarian and look out of place in a garden setting during the daytime, you should conceal these from view as much as possible. You can hide fixtures among thick plantings, beneath a deck overhang, behind a tree trunk, or within a tree canopy. Where such screening is not available, you can recess the fixtures in light wells below ground level. Special light-well fixtures are available. These consist of a bulb and reflector encased in a watertight housing, with a metal grille or clear Plexiglas cover. If you're recessing other types of fixtures below ground level, construct the well so it doesn't fill with water during heavy rains.

Wires and conduit can be buried underground, although junction boxes and transformers for low-voltage systems must be aboveground. In the daytime, fixtures with a black or dark green finish will be less obtrusive in the garden than those with a white or bright metallic finish.

Making a Site Plan

If you've selected a site for the pond and plan to leave the rest of the yard pretty much as it is, a site plan isn't necessary. However, sometimes the pond will be part of a larger landscaping project, which includes adding, removing, or relocating plantings and structures. In that case, it's a good idea to develop a site plan to help you (and others involved in the project) visualize how the pond fits into the overall scheme. The plan can also serve as a guide from which a landscape architect or designer can create finished drawings to submit to the building department, if these are required.

To make the site plan, you'll need to buy some grid paper for a base map (a scale of ¼ inch equal to 1 foot is standard) and some tracing paper for overlays. If you have the original site survey map or site plan for your property, this could also serve as your base map. If you don't have the original map, use a 50-foot tape measure to help measure the size of the lot (or portion being landscaped), and to locate various existing features within it (house, decks, outbuildings, trees, shrubs, etc.). Here is how to proceed:

1 **Marking Property Lines.** On the grid paper, mark the property lines as shown. If only a portion of the property will be affected (the back yard, for instance), you needn't include the entire lot. Indicate north, south, east, and west; also mark the directions of prevailing summer and winter winds. Check with the building department to see how far the pond, or any other added structures, must be set back from lot lines; mark these as dotted lines on your plan.

2 **Locating Existing Structures.** Starting from a front corner of the house (marked X on the drawing), measure the dimensions of the house and transfer them to the plan. Again, if only one yard (front, side, or back) will be affected, you need only

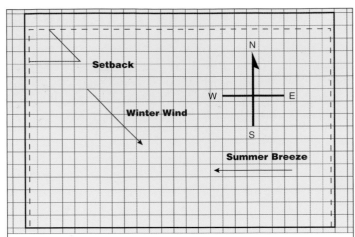

1 Start by drawing a base map on grid paper. Include property lines; north, south, east, and west arrows; property setbacks; and the direction of prevailing winds.

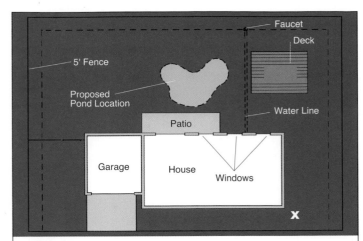

2 Measure the dimensions of the house and any other structures on the property; then transfer them to the plan.

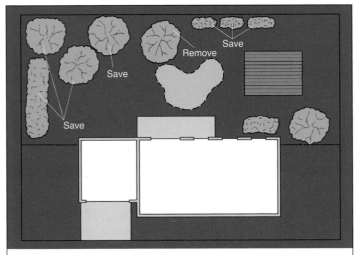

3 Mark locations of all major plantings; note which you want to save and which you want to remove.

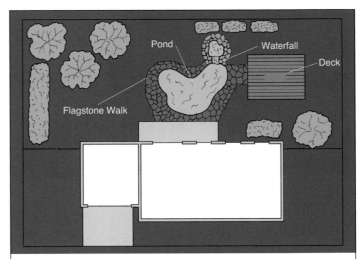

4 Attach a tracing paper overlay to the base plan and draw in any new features, including the pond and coping materials.

show the part of the house that faces it. Include the locations of exterior doors and windows on the wall facing the pond. Measure and mark the locations of other buildings and permanent structures, including patios, decks, fences, and paved walks. Also show any underground or overhead fixtures, such as utility lines and septic systems.

3 Locating Plantings. Mark the locations of trees, shrubs, and other major plantings; then specify which ones are to be kept and which ones will need to be removed or relocated. If applicable, make notations

on the shade cast by trees, tall shrubs, fences, or other structures near the pond site.

4 Locating the Pond on Overlays. On a tracing paper overlay, draw in the exact size and location of the proposed pond. Include coping materials, a waterfall (if one is used), and other features on the pond site, such as walks, planting areas and new plantings, and fountains. Also show the path of new utility lines to the pond.

Use as many overlay sheets as needed to come up with a suitable plan. Draw the final overlay neatly,

and then attach it to the base map. Make copies, if necessary, to show building officials or others involved in the project.

Note: If you're building a raised pond, or one on a sloping site that will be held in place with a retaining wall, you might also want to make one or more cross-sectional drawings. These drawings should include the pond depth, the type and thickness of materials used for the pond sides, the location of any underwater shelves for bog plants, and the location of any required plumbing (pipes, drain, pump, filter, etc.).

pond options

Flexible Pond Liners

Flexible pond liners can be used to create ponds of any shape and size. They offer reasonable cost with ease of installation. As detailed on page 24, you dig the hole for the pond, install the underlayment, lay the liner in the hole, fill the pond with water, cut the liner to size, and then weigh down the exposed edges of the liner with large rocks or other materials to keep it in place. These liners resemble the black polyethylene plastic sheeting sold in hardware stores, but they are much thicker and far more durable. The two most popular types sold today are made of either PVC (polyvinyl chloride) plastic or synthetic (butyl or EPDM) rubber. Both are formulated to be flexible, stretchable, and resistant to ultraviolet light. Rubber liners generally outlast the best of the PVC liners, but they're expensive. The PVC liners are available in thicknesses from 20 to 32 mil. Butyl or EPDM rubber liners are available in thicknesses from 30 to 45 mil. A thicker liner will be more expensive, but it will generally last longer. At the bottom end of the scale, a 20-mil PVC liner can be expected to last from five to seven years; a 32-mil PVC liner will last from ten to 15 years. A rubber liner will generally last from 20 to 30 years. The manufacturer's warranty is a good indicator of liner life. You should choose a thicker liner if you expect uninvited waders, either animal or human, in the pool. (Or apply a 1- to 2-inch layer of cement mortar over the liner to protect it.) If you will be raising fish, make sure you specify a fish-grade liner, because toxic chemicals can leach out of some liners.

Flexible pond liners come in stock sizes ranging from about 5 x 5 feet to 30 x 50 feet. Some manufacturers offer custom sizes, which are priced by the square foot. By joining the edges of the sheets with a seam sealer (available from the liner dealer), you can make a pond of virtually any size. (Indeed, liners have been used to create lakes and reservoirs up to several acres.)

Because flexible liners are susceptible to punctures from rocks, gravel, broken tree roots, or other sharp objects in the pond excavation, installation instructions for plastic and rubber liners often recommend that you should place a layer of sand, carpet padding, or similar cushioning material in the excavation before laying the liner. The main problem with sand, however, is that it doesn't conform well to the steep sidewalls of the pond. Sand is also more expensive and heavy to transport, especially for larger pond excavations. Other

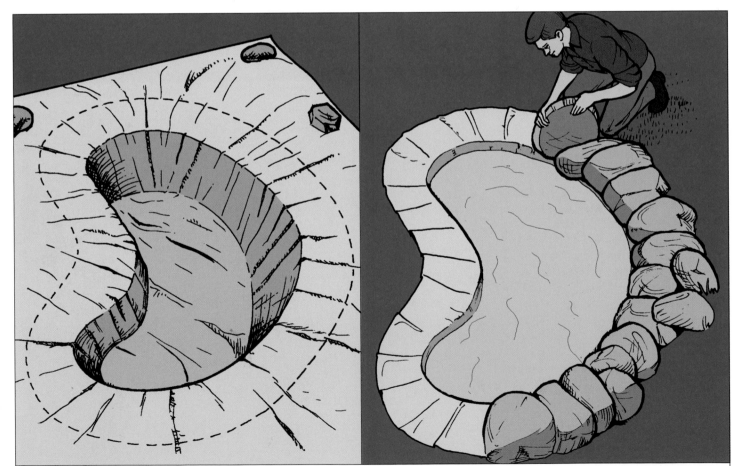

Flexible Pond Liners. Flexible pond liners fit ponds of any shape or size. Boulders or other masonry edging holds the liner in place and hides liner edges above the waterline.

recommended cushioning materials, such as carpet padding or old newspapers, tend to deteriorate over time, losing their cushioning effect. So, most sources that carry pond liners now also offer a tough, yet flexible, underlayment material specifically designed for use with pond liners. A recent product on the market is a thick, synthetic rubber liner with an integral underlayment material bonded to it, to provide a lifetime guarantee against puncture.

If you're digging the hole in soil that contains sharp stones or gravel, protruding tree roots, or soil subject to excessive shifting during winter months, you should install both sand and underlayment fabric. If the soil is stable, fine, and rock-free, however, the underlayment really isn't needed.

Both plastic and rubber liners are useful if you anticipate moving every few years or for other reasons you may have for building a temporary pond. Simply drain the pond and remove the liner. (See page 74 for information on draining ponds.) You can reuse the liner as long as it wasn't covered with cement mortar.

Premolded Pond Shells

Rigid or semi-rigid pond shells are easy to install yourself, as shown on page 34. These shells come in a variety of sizes, shapes, and depths. Although they're generally more expensive than flexible pond liners, they're also more durable and puncture-proof. Shells can last from five to 50 years, depending on their material, thickness, quality, and installation conditions. Generally, the thicker the shell, the longer it will last, and the more expensive it will be. The thickest shells (¼ inch or more) can be installed aboveground with little support around the sides, provided the bottom rests on a firm base. As with most other products, you get what you pay for. The manufacturer's warranty is a good indicator of the durability of a premolded pond shell.

The first preformed pond shells appeared on the market in the mid-1950's, and were made of fiberglass-reinforced polyester (FRP). This is the same material used for fiberglass spas, boat hulls, auto bodies, and translucent roofing panels for patio overheads. Today, more shells are being made of molded plastics, such as ABS (acrylonitrile butadiene styrene) and various polyethylene formulations. The fiberglass shells are usually easier to repair than the plastic ones, but they tend to be more brittle. Whatever shell you buy, though, make sure it is resistant to ultraviolet radiation.

Most manufacturers offer between ten to 15 pond shell designs, in depths from 9 to 18 inches and with capacities from about 30 to 500 gallons. (If you want to raise water lilies, the shell should have a minimum depth of 18 inches.) Keep in mind that the shell will look larger when out of the ground than when installed.

Some shells have integrated premolded waterfall lips; separate premolded waterfall courses are also available. Many preformed shells have shelves or ledges around the edges below the water line for placing shallow-water plants in submersible containers. A few also have depressions around the perimeter for bog plants. You should carefully disguise the edges of the shell with rocks or other materials, so the pool will look natural.

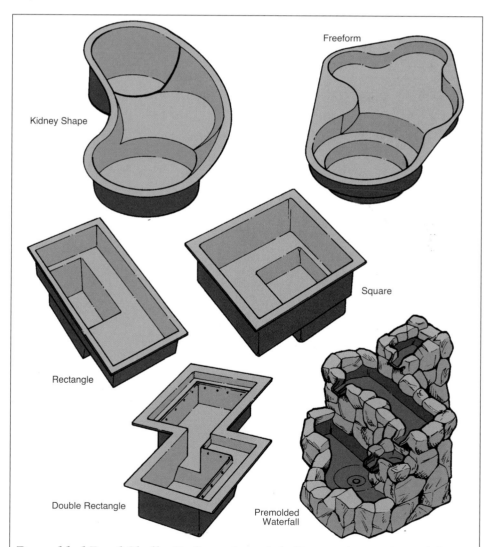

Premolded Pond Shells. Preformed pond shells come in a variety of shapes and sizes. They're the closest thing you can have to an "instant pond".

Kidney Shape

Freeform

Rectangle

Square

Double Rectangle

Premolded Waterfall

Concrete Ponds

Years ago, practically all garden ponds—formal and informal—were made of poured concrete, concrete block, or a combination of the two. With the advent of flexible pool liners and molded pond shells, however, few ponds today are constructed entirely of concrete.

Although a concrete pond can last a lifetime if it is properly installed, it will crack and leak almost immediately if it is not. Success in pouring a concrete pond—even a small one—requires experience with concrete. It is also a lot of back-breaking work. A larger pond, or one with straight or stepped sides, will require extensive formwork. Once a crack opens up, there's usually no way to repair it. The only fix is to cover the concrete with a flexible pool liner. (See page 29.)

Concrete ponds are much more expensive to install than flexible liners or premolded shells, even if you do the work yourself. If you do decide to go with concrete, you should have the pond installed by a local masonry contractor familiar with this sort of construction in your particular climate. The following basic guidelines will help you discuss your plans intelligently with the contractor.

In cold climates, the concrete shell should be at least 6 inches thick and adequately reinforced with ½-inch (No. 2) reinforcing bar or wire mesh to survive the effects of alternate freezing and thawing. (Check local codes for reinforcement requirements.) In milder climates, the shell can be 3 or 4 inches thick, depending on soil conditions.

Since new concrete can leach lime into the pond water, the lime must be neutralized by chemicals; or else you must paint the pond before adding fish and plants. Concrete can be painted with a rubber-based pool paint to create various effects: earthtones for a natural look; white, blue, or turquoise for a more formal appearance; or dark colors for a "bottomless" look.

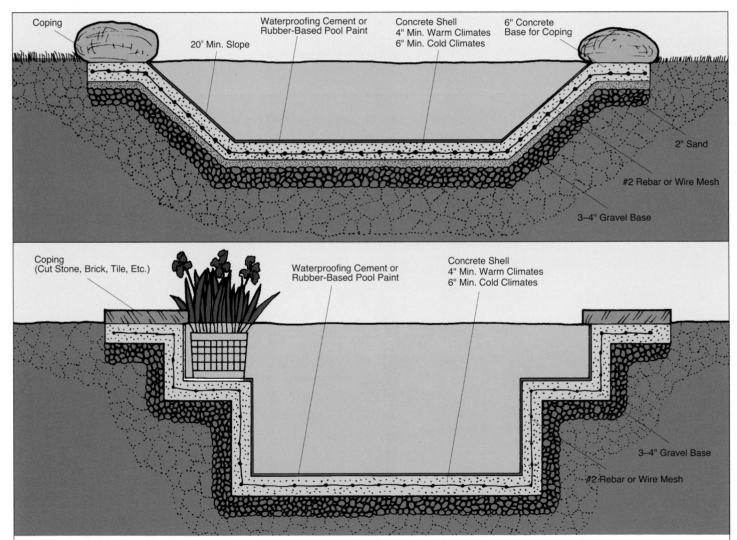

Concrete Ponds. The shell of a concrete pond must be adequately reinforced to prevent cracking. If the sides slope 20 deg. or more from the vertical, no forms are required (top). A formal concrete pond with straight sides requires extensive formwork that is best left to a professional installer (bottom).

Other Options

Pond Kits. Some manufacturers offer complete pond kits. These include a rigid shell or flexible liner with a matched pump, filter, and—in some cases—a fountainhead or self-contained waterfall, planting containers, and pond-treatment chemicals for the initial startup. If you find a design you like, the kits are much easier to install successfully than separate components, because everything is guaranteed to work together. Such kits are usually limited to smaller ponds, however.

Tub Gardens. If you want to have a small-scale water garden without the trouble of building a pond, you can raise a few water plants and small fish in large containers. Tub gardens make wonderful accents for decks, patios, porches, and planting beds. Prefabricated water-garden containers are available up to 36 inches in diameter; half-barrels also make good containers when lined with a flexible plastic or rubber liner, as do large terra-cotta or plastic pots, or

any other large, rustproof, watertight vessel. Many people have even made successful water gardens in old clawfoot bathtubs! You could also use a large wooden planter box; just install a plastic or rubber liner, and fill it with water.

Pond Depth & Capacity

The most successful garden ponds are between 18 and 24 inches deep. Very small ponds (5 to 10 square feet) can be as shallow as 12 inches; very large ponds (500 square feet or more) can be up to 36 inches deep. The 18- to 24-inch depth is considered optimum for growing water lilies and other aquatic plants; this is sufficient, too, for raising most types of fish and other aquatic life. Also, except in the coldest climates, a depth of 24 inches is sufficient to prevent the pond from freezing all the way to the bottom, and killing fish or damaging the pond shell as a result. If you live in an area with extremely harsh winters, contact the local pond

builders in your area for recommended depths.

If you're installing a Japanese koi pond, you may need to provide an area at least 3 feet deep where fish can escape heat in the summer and frozen water in the winter. (See page 71.) Small, shallow ponds (less than 18 inches deep) heat up and cool off more quickly than large, deep ones. These extreme temperature changes can stress fish. Shallow ponds are also more subject to excess algae growth during hot weather. In extremely cold climates, they may freeze all the way to the bottom, killing plants and fish. However, some plants (especially bog plants) may require water more shallow than the recommended depth. In such cases, you can create a shelf around the pond perimeter to raise water plants. Or, you can put the plants in containers and elevate them off the pond bottom with bricks or stones as discussed on page 68. (For more information on stocking the pond with plants and fish, see page 67.)

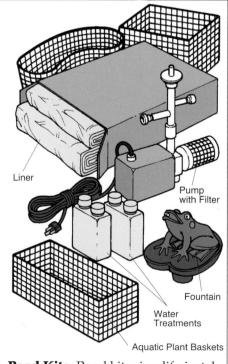

Pond Kits. Pond kits simplify installation with matched components and easy-to-follow instructions.

Liner

Pump with Filter

Fountain

Water Treatments

Aquatic Plant Baskets

Tub Gardens. Old bathtubs, plastic or terra-cotta pots, and wooden planter boxes are just some of the imaginative ways you can create a container water garden.

Pond Capacity

The pond capacity (in gallons of water) becomes important when you size the pump and filter and when you determine correct dosages of plant fertilizers, fish medications, algaecides, and other chemical treatments. The most accurate way to determine pond capacity is to attach a flow meter to the faucet or water-supply line, and then to simply record the number of gallons needed to fill the pond. A less accurate, but easier and less expensive method, is as follows: Turn on the garden hose at a steady flow rate, and time how long it takes to fill a 5-gallon bucket (say, 10 seconds). Then time how many minutes it takes to fill the pond at the same flow rate (say, 20 minutes). Now figure out the flow rate of the hose in gallons per minute (5 gallons @ 10 seconds x 6 = 30 gallons per minute). Next, multiply the gallons per minute by the number of minutes it took to fill the pond (30 gallons x 20 minutes = 600 gallons).

If it isn't practical to fill the pond with water, you can calculate capacity using one of the following formulas, assuming the pond sides are straight (or steeply sloped) and the bottom is flat (not bowl-shaped).

Rectilinear ponds. If the pond is roughly square or rectangular, measure its average depth, width, and length; then multiply the three figures to determine cubic feet (D x W x L = cubic feet). Multiply the cubic feet by 7.5 to get capacity in gallons.

Circular ponds. To calculate the capacity of circular ponds, use this formula: diameter x diameter (diameter squared) x depth x 5.9 = gallons.

Oval ponds. To calculate the capacity of oval ponds, use this formula: depth x width x length x 6.7 = gallons.

Freeform ponds. It is tough to accurately calculate the volume of an irregularly shaped pond. The best way is to determine the average width and length, and then use the equation for oval ponds above.

The Pond Bottom

No matter what material your pond will be made of, or what surface shape it takes, steep sloping sides are preferable to a shallow bowl shape. Not only will a pond made this way hold more water, but it will also look better. In very large ponds, you may want to include shallow areas for raising plants or viewing fish. In all cases, the pond bottom should not be perfectly flat. Slope it slightly toward a sump hole to trap dirt and debris, and also to facilitate cleaning. In some ponds, the sump contains a drain or submersible pump to improve water circulation.

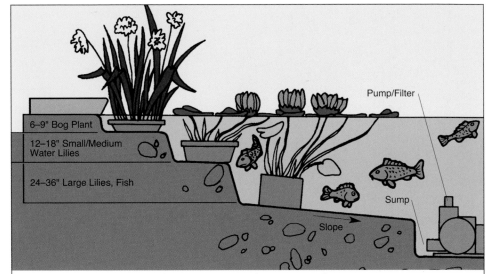

6–9" Bog Plant

12–18" Small/Medium Water Lilies

24–36" Large Lilies, Fish

Pump/Filter

Sump

Slope

The Pond Bottom. Shelves around the edge of the pond provide proper depths for various types of water plants; the bottom slopes toward the sump to simplify cleaning.

Local Codes & Pond Safety

Any body of water, no matter how shallow, poses a hazard for infants and small children. Many communities have zoning ordinances that require a wall or fence around ponds over a certain size or depth (usually 18 inches deep), to keep neighborhood children from straying into the pond area. If you have infants or toddlers in the family, consider encircling the pond area with a temporary wire fence and locking gate. Or you might want to postpone pond construction altogether, until the children are old enough to learn water-safety rules. Remember, too, it is your responsibility to make sure that neighborhood children don't have access to your pond—whether this means a fence around the pond or your entire yard.

Your local building department may have additional codes and requirements for the size and design of the pond itself; in some cases, a building permit and inspection may be required. If you're running electricity to the pond for a pump and/or lighting, you may need a separate electrical permit. Many communities require that a licensed electrician must perform any electrical work involving water or outdoor wiring. We highly recommend this practice, even if local codes don't require it. Be sure to choose an electrician with experience in this type of work. For referrals, local swimming pool contractors are a good source.

flexible liners

Sizing the Liner

Flexible pond liners come in a variety of stock sizes, with larger sizes available as special orders. Some garden suppliers carry large rolls of liner material in standard widths: You simply pull as much off the roll as required. Here's how to estimate the amount of liner you need.

1 Outlining the Shape. After clearing the site of plantings and other obstructions, outline the pond shape on the ground. For irregularly shaped ponds, use a rope or garden hose to mark the pond perimeter. For squares or rectangles, use batter boards, stakes, and string, and employ the "3-4-5" triangulation method to make sure all corners meet at an exact 90-degree angle. From each corner, measure along one string a distance of 3 feet; along the other string, measure a distance of 4 feet; then mark these locations on the strings with chalk or a piece of tape. Adjust the strings on the batter boards until the diagonal distance between the two points measures 5 feet.

For circular ponds, make a simple "compass" with a stake; sturdy twine or rope; and a sharpened stick, screwdriver, or other pointed object. Scribe the outline of the pond in the dirt, and mark it with flour, powdered gypsum, marking paint, or a garden hose.

2 Measuring Pond Dimensions. Measure the overall width and length of the pond; then determine the smallest rectangle that would enclose the pond area.

3 Calculating the Liner. To allow for pond depth, decide on the maximum depth of the pond (usually 24 inches), double it, and add this figure to the width and length of the rectangle. To allow for overlap, add an additional 24 inches to the width and length of the liner. This will provide

1 Outline the shape of the pond on the ground. For irregular shapes, use a garden hose or rope; for square or rectangular ponds, use batter boards and string; for round ponds, use a rope, stake, and pointed stick as a giant compass.

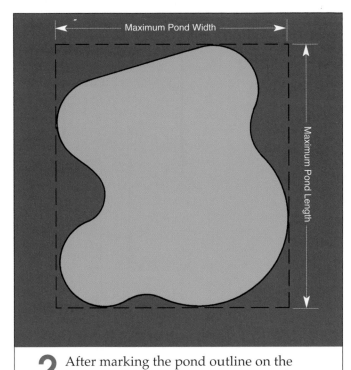

2 After marking the pond outline on the ground, measure the maximum width and length of the pond.

3 Add twice the pond depth to each dimension, plus 2 ft. This will be the liner size.

12 inches of overlap around the pond rim once the liner is installed.

Example: The pond is 24 inches deep and fits inside a 10x12-foot rectangle. To figure liner width, add 10 feet (the width), plus 4 feet (the depth, doubled), plus 2 feet (for overlap)—for a total of 16 feet. To figure the liner length, add 12 feet (the length), plus 4 feet (the depth, doubled), plus 2 feet—for a total of 18 feet. You would therefore need a 16x18-foot liner for a 10x12-foot pond. Note that for irregularly shaped ponds, you may need to trim excess liner material to provide an even overlap around the entire pond.

Installing the Liner

Installing a vinyl liner requires four basic steps: first, digging the hole; second, laying down the liner; third, filling the pond with water; and fourth, adding stones or other edging around the pond perimeter. The actual procedure, however, involves a few more steps than listed above. These are presented on the following pages. Depending on your particular requirements, you may be able to skip a few of these steps.

1 **Removing Sod.** If you've located the pond in a lawn area, use a flat shovel to remove patches or strips of sod within the pond area, and about 6 to 12 inches beyond the perimeter. Reestablish the pond outline, if necessary.

1 If the pond is in a lawn area, remove the sod within the pond area and about 6 to 12 in. beyond it.

2 If the pond will have shallow-water shelves, dig the pond to the depth of the shelves; tamp the shelf area with a tamper; then dig the deep area of the pond.

2 Digging Shelves for Shallow-Water Plants. This step is optional. If the pond will include shelves around the perimeter for bog plants, excavate for these. Typically, shallow-water shelves are about 12 to 16 inches wide and 9 to 12 inches below the top edge of the excavation. First, excavate the entire pond area to the depth of the shelf; then use a tamping tool to compact the soil firmly in the shelf area (hand and power tampers are available at tool rental shops). Use a straight board and 2-foot level to make sure the shelf is level around the entire perimeter of the pond. Then excavate the remainder of the pond down to the maximum depth, sloping the sides as described in step 3.

3 Digging the Hole. Start by digging around the shelf perimeter to the depth of the shovel blade (9 to 12 inches); then remove all dirt within the pond area, by layers, to the final depth. Check the depth frequently with a tape measure or yardstick and long board placed over the hole, as shown. The sides should slope inward at about a 20-degree angle from the vertical; in loose or sandy soil, the sides may have to conform to a shallower slope. Slope the bottom of the excavation about 1/2- to 1-inch per foot toward the center or toward one end; at the lowest point, dig a shallow (6- to 8-inch) sump hole to facilitate draining the pond.

4 Cutting Ledge for Edging Material. With a flat-blade shovel, cut a 12- to 15-inch-wide ledge around the pond rim to provide a flat, level surface on which to install the edging materials. Cut the ledge to a depth that will accommodate the combined thickness of the edging and any underlayment materials. (If you're mortaring the stones in place, be sure to include the thickness of a mortar bed—about 2 to 3 inches.) As shown, the edging should extend at least 1 inch above the surrounding terrain to prevent runoff from entering the pond. Also keep in mind that edging looks best if it overhangs the pond edges by a few inches.

3 Dig the hole to the proper depth. As you dig, check the depth with a long, straight board and tape measure.

4 Use a flat-blade shovel to cut a ledge around the pond perimeter for coping.

5 For small ponds, use a 2x4 and a level to level the pond edges as shown here. For larger ponds, drive stakes around the pond perimeter and level the stake tops.

6 Pack sand into the excavation to cushion the liner. Underlayment may also be used.

5 Checking Edges for Level. Once the pond is filled with water, the water level will quickly reveal any high or low spots around the pond rim. For small ponds, place a long, straight 2x4 across the pond excavation, with each end resting on the edging ledge. Place a level on top of the board; then move the board to various points across the length and width of the pond while checking the level. If necessary, cut down high spots on the ledge (or build up low ones) until the entire pond rim is level.

To check a large pond, drive short stakes or pegs 3 to 4 feet apart around the rim of the pond; then level the tops of the stakes with a long spirit level, or a short level placed on top of a straight board. Measure how much each stake protrudes from the ground. If the same length of each stake protrudes, you know the perimeter is level.

6 Preparing the Hole. Carefully inspect the excavation for any sharp stones or projecting roots, and remove them. Place carpet padding or a 2- to 3-inch cushion of damp sand in the bottom of the

excavation and on any shelves cut into the sides of the pond. Also pack damp sand into any voids in the sidewalls, such as where large rocks were removed. If the soil is very rocky or infested with roots, lay down a fabric underlayment material for additional protection. (See page 18.)

7 Positioning the Liner. Pick a warm, sunny day to install the liner. To make it more flexible and easier to handle, warm up the liner for a few minutes by spreading it out on sun-warmed pavement. With a helper (or two), drape the liner loosely into the excavation, with an even overlap on all sides; then

7 Drape the liner over the hole, and weight down the edges with rocks. Begin filling the pond with water.

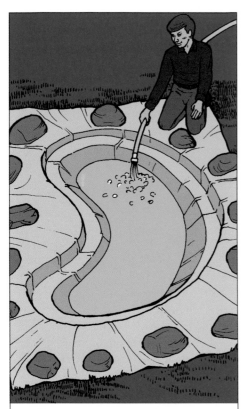

8 As the pond fills, stretch the liner to remove any wrinkles; fold excess liner into neat pleats. Ease off the stones as the water pulls the liner into the hole.

weight down the edges with a few smooth, flat stones or bricks. Avoid dragging the liner across the ground, since this may cause a puncture. Once the liner is in place, start filling the pond with water.

8 **Fitting the Liner.** As the pond fills with water, adjust the liner to conform to the sides of the pond; smooth out as many creases and wrinkles as possible. Large creases at tight corners can be stretched out and pleated to make them less noticeable. As the pond fills, periodically ease off the stone weights to avoid overstretching the liner.

9 **Trimming Excess Lining.** When the pond is full, trim off excess lining with a heavy pair of scissors or a utility knife. Leave enough liner around the pond rim to extend underneath, and a few inches behind, the first course of edging stones. To keep the liner in place while adding edging, push 20d nails through the liner into the ground every foot or so around the pond rim.

10 **Adding Edging Materials.** If you're using natural stones (boulders or flagstone, for example), make several trial arrangements until you find one that looks most natural. Although large, flat stones or masonry units can be placed directly over the liner, you must position them carefully so they won't slip into the pond. It's usually better to set the stones in a 2- to 3-inch-thick mortar bed (reinforced with chicken wire or metal lath). You can buy mortar premixed, or make your own mix. Typically, a mix consists of 1 part cement, ¼ part hydrated lime, and 3 parts sand by volume. If you expect frequent foot traffic on the edging, pour a 4-inch-thick base of reinforced concrete under the stones. Allow the mortar to cure (about one week); next, scrub the edging with distilled vinegar to neutralize the lime in the mortar. Then drain the pond, rinse the liner, and refill the pond with fresh water. (See page 74 for information on draining ponds.)

9 When the pond is full, secure the edges of the liner with large nails. Use scissors to cut off excess liner. Save cut pieces for future repairs.

10 Place coping stones around the edge of the pond. To prevent stones from moving, mortar them in place.

Liner Over Concrete. In certain situations, concrete can be combined with a flexible plastic or rubber pond liner to provide the best of both materials. For example, you can pour a concrete retainer around the sidewalls of the pond to provide additional support for liners—especially in loose or crumbly soil, where the walls tend to break down because of soil slippage behind the liner. A concrete retainer allows you to have steeper walls and to place large or heavy pots on the shallow-water shelves. Because the liner acts as a watertight barrier, the concrete itself needn't be waterproof. Furthermore, minor cracks in the concrete shell won't result in leaks. You can also use liners in conjunction with a thick, concrete perimeter footing or collar. This will support heavy rocks around the pond perimeter, or it will serve as a base for a brick or stone patio or walk around the pond.

When you excavate for the pond, allow extra space for building wooden forms (if required) for the concrete retainers and footings. If you're not experienced here, you should hire a masonry contractor to do the work. For more information on mixing and pouring concrete, refer to "Quick Guide: Patios & Walks."

Cement Over Liner. A thin layer of a plastic cement mixture (1 part plastic cement to 4 parts sand) placed over the liner will protect it from the damaging effects of ultraviolet rays, as well as punctures caused by waders in the pond. Plastic cement has latex additives that make it highly resistant to cracking. (Most lumber yards and masonry suppliers carry this product.) If you want, you can add coloring agents to the cement and/or produce various surface textures by brooming or troweling. After installing the flexible liner (see page 25), you should cover it

with a chicken-wire reinforcement; then you hand-pack a 1-inch layer of cement over the entire surface of the pond (wear heavy gloves for this procedure). Start packing cement at the base of the sidewall, building up to the top in 6-foot-long sections. After the sidewalls are covered, do the pond bottom. Brush or trowel the surface smooth; then allow the cement to harden (about 10 to 12 hours, or overnight). Once the cement has hardened, fill the pond with water. Add 1 gallon of distilled white vinegar per 100 gallons of water, and allow this mixture to stand one week. (The vinegar serves to neutralize the lime leaching from the cement.) Drain the pond; rinse it thoroughly; then refill the pond with fresh water. (See page 74 for infomation on draining a pond.) Test the water for pH (see page 63) before adding fish or plants. If the water is too alkaline, repeat the vinegar treatment.

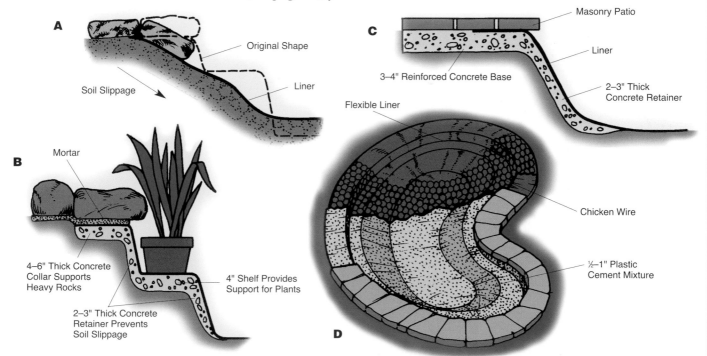

A. In loose or sandy soil, slippage causes walls to break down. **B.** A concrete retainer prevents soil slippage and provides support for heavy coping and plant shelves. **C.** A concrete base provides support for a pond-side masonry patio or walk. **D.** A thin (1-inch) layer of plastic cement protects flexible liner from UV rays and punctures.

3 Flexible Liners

Building a Raised Pond with a Flexible Liner

Flexible liners also adapt well to raised-pond enclosures. The supporting sidewalls can be wood, mortared bricks, concrete blocks, or any other material that provides firm support for the liner. You can build masonry enclosures on a simple concrete perimeter footing. (Check local codes for the footing depths.) Or you can install a wooden frame directly on the ground. In both cases, the pond bottom needs to be nothing

more than 1 or 2 inches of compacted damp sand or finely sifted soil to protect the liner from punctures. If you make a wooden frame, use pressure-treated wood or redwood to prevent rot. Avoid boards with rough, splintery surfaces, which could puncture the liner.

The raised pond shown here is a 6x8-foot wooden box, approximately 20 inches tall. It will provide a water depth of about 16 inches. Each side is made of two 2x10 boards. By changing the width and

number of boards used to make the sides, you can change the pond depth, although for practical purposes the depth shouldn't exceed 24 inches. Also, the length and width should not exceed about 8 feet, or the boards may bow outward from the weight of the water.

1 Making the Sides. Cut the four 1x4 middle battens to 17 inches long. Place two 2x10x 8-foot side pieces together as shown. Center a batten across the side pieces, with the bottom of the batten flush to the bottom of one of the boards. Attach the batten with 2-inch galvanized deck screws. Repeat for all four sides.

2 Joining the Sides. Select a level site for your pond, and join the sides in place. Join the sides with four 3½-inch galvanized deck screws in each corner. Lap the long sides over the ends of the short sides. Be sure the corners are flush at the top, and drive the screws below the surface of the wood. Set a carpenter's level on top of a long

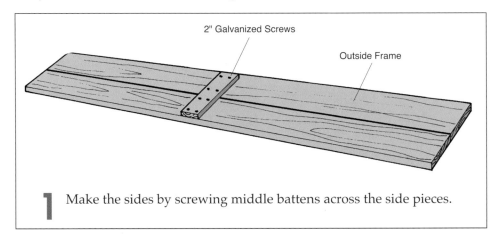

1 Make the sides by screwing middle battens across the side pieces.

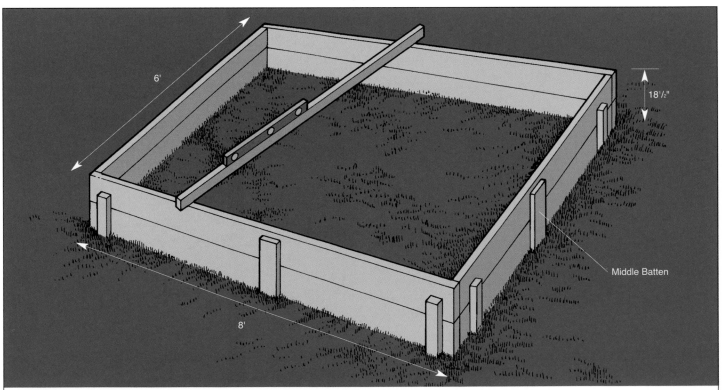

2 Join the sides with butt joints at the corners. Level and square the frame.

Temporary Stakes Still in Place

3 Fill the liner with water, and secure the edges with 1x2 battens and 4d galvanized box nails.

4 Attach wider corner batten over the shorter sides and the narrower battens over the longer sides.

straight board, and use it to check for level across the frame. Measure across the diagonals of the frame. If the measurements of both diagonals are the same, the frame is square. After the frame is square and level, drive stakes into the ground at each outside corner; then temporarily screw the stakes to the frame to hold it in position. With medium-grit sandpaper or a rasp, lightly round over any sharp edges on the pond rim.

3 Installing the Liner. Carefully check the ground within the frame for any sharp rocks, projecting roots, or other sharp objects, and remove these. Backfill inside the frame with 1 to 2 inches of sand or finely sifted soil. (You may use a liner underlayment material in lieu of sand; see page 18.) Loosely drape the liner into the box, keeping an even overlap on all sides. Then slowly fill the pond with water, lightly stretching and folding the wrinkles into neat creases as the water level rises. Take care not to overstretch the liner. When the water level is about 6 inches below the top edge of the box, shut off the water. Wrap the liner edge over the top of the pond, and secure the edges with 1x2 battens and 4d galvanized box nails, as shown. Trim the liner along the bottom of the 1x2 battens with a utility knife.

4 Attaching the Corner Battens. Each corner has a 1x4 batten (actually $3\frac{1}{2}$ inches wide) that laps over the edge of a 1x2$\frac{3}{4}$-inch batten. This way, the width of the corner looks the same on both sides. Work on one corner at a time. Remove the temporary stake and attach the corner battens with 2-inch galvanized decking screws. Attach the wider battens over the shorter sides and the narrower battens over the longer sides. This will stagger the butt joints at the corner, making the corners stronger.

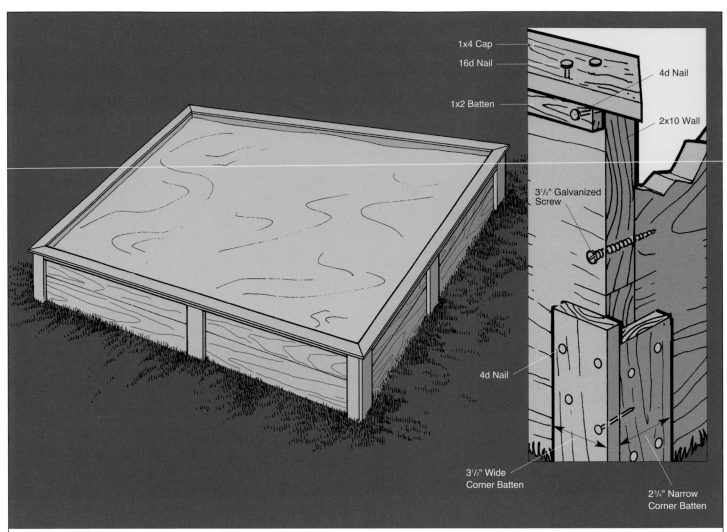

1x4 Cap

16d Nail

1x2 Batten

4d Nail

2x10 Wall

3½" Galvanized Screw

4d Nail

3½" Wide Corner Batten

2¾" Narrow Corner Batten

5 Attach the mitered top pieces with 16d nails into the top of the sides and 4d nails into the horizontal battens.

5 Cutting and Attaching Cap Pieces. Cut the cap pieces to the lengths in the Materials List, with a 45-degree miter at each end. Nail the cap pieces into the top side pieces with 16d galvanized common nails, and into the horizontal battens with 4d nails galvanized finishing nails.

Materials List

Qty.	Part	Lumber
4	Long Walls	2x10x8'
4	Short Walls	2x10x69"
4	Middle Battens	1x4x17"
2	Long Battens	1x2x8'
2	Short Battens	1x2x73½"
4	Wide Corner Battens	1x4x17"
4	Narrow Corner Battens	1x2³/₄x17"
2	Long Cap Pieces	1x4x8'2"
2	Short Cap Pieces	1x4x74"

rigid liners

Basic Requirements

The ground in which you install the pond must be firm, stable, and free of rocks, projecting roots, and other sharp objects. Also, the shell must be fully supported by firm, well-packed earth in the excavation. Because a shell full of water can weigh up to several tons, any voids or bumps underneath may cause the shell to crack or buckle. In extremely loose or sandy soil, ground water can cause erosion around the shell, creating voids that will weaken it. Similarly, frost heaving in cold climates can deform or buckle the shell. If you anticipate either of these conditions, make the excavation about 6 to 8 inches deeper and wider than the shell. Next, backfill the hole with 3 to 4 inches of smooth pea gravel, topped with 2 inches of finely sifted soil; then tamp firmly. If you plan to place a statuary fountain, boulders, or other heavy objects in the pond, you may want to pour a concrete slab in the bottom of the excavation to support the additional weight before you install the shell.

Shell Installation

1 **Marking the Shell Outline.** Place the preformed shell upright in the desired location. Use plumbed stakes or a plumb bob to transfer the shape of the pond rim to the ground, and mark the outline with a rope or garden hose. Use stakes (spaced about 12 inches apart) to keep the hose or rope in place.

2 **Digging the Hole.** Excavate the hole to conform to the shape of the pond shell, allowing an extra 2 inches around the pond perimeter and 2 to 3 inches in the bottom of the hole. If the shell has shallow-water shelves, cut ledges at the appropriate locations to support them. The thinner shells, in particular, must be fully supported at all points. Remove any rocks or other sharp objects; then line the bottom of the hole with 2 to 3 inches of damp sand or finely sifted soil. (For thinner shells, you may also want to use an underlayment fabric; see page 18.) Flatten the bottom of the hole with a short board or screed, and then firmly tamp the soil to provide a stable base for the shell. Make sure the bottom of the excavation is perfectly level in all directions. You can do this with a 4-foot spirit level, or a shorter level placed on a 2x4 laid on the sand base.

3 **Setting the Shell.** With a helper, set the pond shell into the excavation, and check the height of the rim. It should be about 1 inch above the surrounding ground to prevent runoff from entering the pond. Add or remove soil from the bottom of the hole as necessary to achieve the desired height.

4 **Leveling the Shell.** Place a long, straight 2x4 across the shell rim in several places, and check with a level. If the shell isn't

1 Set the shell in position. Use leveled stakes and a garden hose to transfer the pond shape to the ground, as shown.

2 Dig a hole slightly larger than the shell; then backfill with damp sand. Use a short board to level the bottom of the excavation.

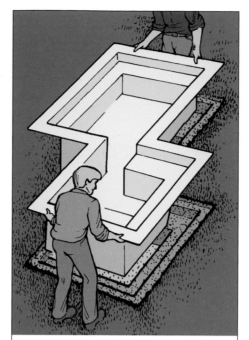

3 With a helper, lift the shell and lower it into the excavation.

4 Place a long 2x4 and level across the top of the shell in several locations to level it. Add more sand to support the bottom of the shell, if necessary.

level, pull it out of the hole and re-level the excavation as necessary. Just make sure the pond is perfectly level before you fill it with water. Even a few inches of water in the pond bottom will make the shell virtually impossible to move.

5 **Backfilling Around the Pond.**
After the shell is leveled, slowly fill it with water. As the water level rises, backfill the hole around the shell with sifted dirt or damp sand, tamping it gently with a shovel handle or the end of a 2x4. Make sure you fill all voids, especially around any shallow-water shelves. Check the rim for level frequently as you go. Do not allow the water level inside the pond to rise above the backfilled earth outside the rim, or else the shell will tend to bulge outward. In other words, try to equalize the pressure exerted on both sides of the shell as you backfill around it.

5 Slowly fill the shell with water, backfilling around the pond edges as the water level rises. Check frequently with a level.

6 Adding Coping. When the shell is filled with water, you can conceal the exposed rim with rocks, masonry materials, or overhanging plants. If you are using flagstones or flat pavers, allow them to overhang the pond edges by 1 to 2 inches. Don't allow the full weight of the edging to rest on the pond rim, because its weight may deform or damage the pond walls. Instead, embed the edging in a 3- to 4-inch-thick bed of mortar, raised slightly above the lip of the shell. After the mortar cures (in about one week), scrub the coping with distilled vinegar to neutralize the lime in the mortar. Then drain the pond, rinse it, and refill it with fresh water. (See page 74 for information on draining a pond.)

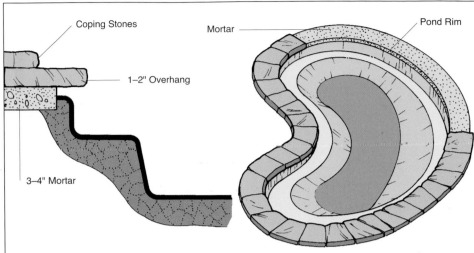

6 Place coping stones around the edges, overhanging them slightly to hide the shell rim. For a more permanent installation, mortar the stones in place.

Building a Raised Pond with a Preformed Shell

Some of the thickest shells can be installed freestanding, with only a thin, decorative skirt of wood, brick, or masonry block to support the rim. Thinner shells will require additional support—usually earth or concrete backfill—between the wall and the pond shell. Check with the shell manufacturer or dealer for the recommended application for the shell you've chosen. Follow the same backfilling procedure as for in-ground ponds. (See page 35.) The drawings show details for a partially raised pond and a fully raised pond. For a partially raised pond, sink the lower part of the shell up to the shelf level.

Then build the wall from ground level up to the lip of the pond, backfilling behind the wall as you go (if required). If you are using brick, stone, or concrete blocks, you'll need to pour a footing to support the wall, as shown. Make the footing at least twice the width of the wall and a minimum of 4 inches deep. (In cold climates, deeper footings may be required; check local codes.) Build the wall up to the pond lip; then you can use mortar edging or cap stones over the lip to hide it, as shown.

Fully raised shells require a firm foundation. You can't install them on loose or shifting soil because this settling of the soil beneath will crack or buckle the shell. To play it safe, install the pond on a reinforced concrete slab. Make the slab large enough to support both the shell and the outside supporting wall. The slab should be a minimum of 4 inches thick, with thickened edges (typically 6 inches thick) to support the wall. In cold climates, you may need to add a perimeter footing that extends below the frost line. Reinforce the slab with ½-inch reinforcement bars (rebar), spaced on a 12-inch grid; or use wire-reinforcing mesh. Check local codes for recommendations. In addition to the outside wall, install a second interior wall of bricks or concrete blocks to support the shallow-water shelves. Try to sandwich carpet padding or liner underlayment material between the shell and supporting masonry surfaces.

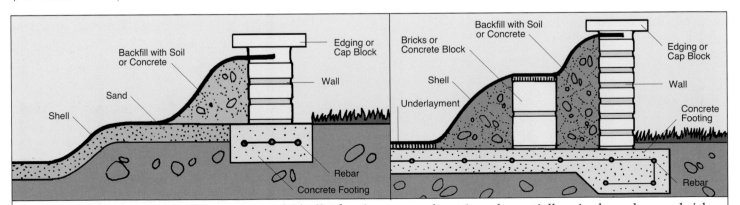

Building a Raised Pond with a Preformed Shell. The aboveground portion of a partially raised pond uses a brick skirt to conceal the shell (left). A fully raised pond requires firm support around the edges and underneath the shell. Backfill voids with tamped soil or concrete (right).

falls & streams

Planning Pointers

Waterfalls can imitate the streams and cascades found in nature, or they can be formal in design. Natural-looking watercourses use rocks of various sizes: from large boulders to create a cascading effect, to smaller stones and pebbles placed in the watercourse itself. For formal ponds, you can incorporate timbers, poured concrete slabs, precast concrete basins, masonry blocks or bricks, or even ceramic tiles. In both formal and informal ponds, waterfalls usually consist of a series of small pools or catch basins linked by low cascades. If space is limited, you can install a single raised basin above the pond, connected by a single fall; or you can have the falls gush spring-like from a fissure in a rock wall or ledge above the pond. If space permits, you could include a meandering stream between the falls.

Building a successful watercourse is largely a matter of trial and error. To create the effect you want, you'll have to experiment with different sizes and shapes of rocks, as well as their placement in and around the watercourse. Before starting, try to have a good idea of the effect you want to create. Look at as many photographs of waterfalls as you can find. Take hikes along local streams, noting the size, shape, and texture of the rocks, and how the water moves over and around them. Study public and private man-made streams and waterfalls in your area. If possible, ask landscape architects and designers to show you their work. When observing man-made water features, find out the type and size of pump used to produce the effect.

Design your waterfall so all water drops directly into the pool or catch basin beneath it; large amounts of water will be lost if water is allowed to splash outside catch basins or the pond. Keeping the falls low and the watercourse relatively short will minimize water loss through evaporation. Smaller, deep basins are preferable to larger, shallow ones, too, for keeping evaporation to a minimum. Also, you must build the watercourse carefully to avoid leaks between rocks along the bank and behind the falls.

Planning Pointers. The most effective waterfalls consist of a series of small pools connected by short cascades.

Sizing the Waterfall

You should keep the waterfall in scale with the pond. A small trickle in a large pond won't be very dramatic, and it will be relatively ineffective in recirculating and oxygenating the water. On the other hand, a large cascade gushing into a small pond will disrupt a large portion of the water surface, stirring up sediment and making it nearly impossible to raise fish, water lilies, and other aquatic plants that prefer still water. If you want both a large, cascading fall and aquatic plants, you should design the pond so that plants can be placed away from the wave action and splashing.

Choosing a Pump

Recirculated water from the pond supplies the running water in a waterfall or fountain. This is accomplished by a small electric pump. A variety of pumps made specifically for ponds are available from water-garden suppliers and local swimming-pool dealers. When choosing a pump, the first step is to select a size that will provide enough flow to operate the waterfall or other water feature in your pond. Beyond sizing, you must decide whether or not you want a submersible (in-pond) pump or one located outside the pond. Other considerations are the overall pump quality and durability. Let's start with sizing.

Sizing the Pump

In general, a pump that recirculates one half of the pond's total water volume per hour will provide the minimum flow required to produce a pleasing proportion of moving water for the size of the pond. For example, if the pond holds 1,000 gallons of water, you should select a pump that will deliver at least 500 gallons per hour (gph) at the top of the falls. For a larger, bolder cascade, select a pump that will turn over the total gallonage of the pond in one hour.

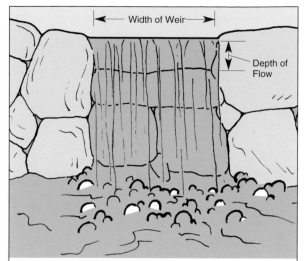

Sizing the Pump. For a heavy (1-in.) depth of flow over the weir, allow 150 gallons per hour for each inch of width; for a light (¼-in.) depth of flow, allow 50 gal. per hour for each inch of width.

Pump Performance. Pump performance is determined by the amount of water the pump can deliver at various heights above water level. Pump makers provide this information in their performance data. For best performance, locate the pump near the base of falls.

Another way to determine the pump size is to directly calculate the amount of water required for cascades of various sizes. First measure the width of the spillway over which the water will flow (called the weir). Then decide how deep you want the water where it flows over the weir. For a light sheet of water (¼-inch deep), allow 50 gallons per hour for each inch of weir. For a heavy flow (1 inch deep), allow 150 gallons per hour for each inch of weir. For example, if the falls will be 6 inches wide, you'll need a pump that can deliver 300 gph for a ¼-inch-deep flow. It will deliver 900 gph for a 1-inch-deep flow.

Pump Performance. When shopping for a pump, check the performance charts that come with the product. Most pumps are rated in gallons per hour at a height of 1 foot above the water surface. The charts also list the amount of water delivered at various heights above the pump. This height is referred to as "head" or "lift." The higher you place the discharge for the waterfall above the pond, the lower the pump output. For example, a pump that delivers 300 gallons at a 1-foot head may deliver only 120 gallons at a 4-foot head.

In their performance charts, the manufacturers also provide a maximum head figure, which is the theoretical maximum height to which the pump can lift water. In practice, the amount of water delivered near or at the maximum head will be reduced to a trickle. Also, the actual maximum head might be lower than the theoretical maximum, depending on how the pump is installed. Some pumps are designed with a low flow and high maximum head, whereas others of the same size are designed with a high flow but a low maximum head. For best pump performance, keep the total height of the falls well below the maximum head height. A total height of 2 to 3 feet above the pond surface should be enough for a visually pleasing waterfall (or series of falls) while optimizing pump performance.

Positioning the Pump. Placing the recirculating pump or pump inlet close to the falls will increase the pump efficiency, because less tubing or pipe will be required between the pump and the head of the falls. As a rule of thumb, every 10 feet of horizontal pipe or tubing is equal to 1 foot of vertical rise in reducing the performance of the pump. A filter added to the system will also restrict flow. If you want to incorporate a fountain in addition to the waterfall, add the gallons per hour required to operate the fountain to your overall figure. Consult your pump supplier for details.

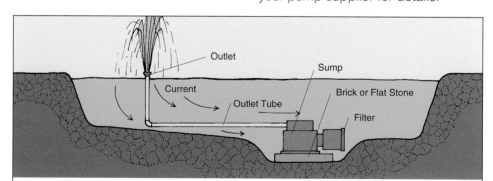

Positioning the Pump. If the pump will be used for filtration only, place the pump/filter at the deepest part of the pond. Or, in a sump, run the outlet tube to the opposite side of the pond for increased water circulation. Raise the pump/filter a few inches off the pond bottom to prevent frequent clogging of the filter.

If the pump will be used for filtration only (no waterfall or fountain included), arrange the system so that the pump intake is at one end of the pond and the discharge is at the other. This will produce a slight current across the bottom of the pond, which will aid in recirculating the water to remove sediment and other water impurities. Usually, you place the pump intake at the deepest part of the pond, and then you design the pond so that a slight current moves the sediment to this point. If you're using a submersible pump, raise it 2 or 3 inches off the pond bottom by setting it on a few bricks or flat stones to prevent silt and other sediment from clogging the pump intake. Most pumps have built-in strainers to prevent leaves and other heavy debris from clogging the pump.

Buy a pump slightly larger than you think you'll need. You can always restrict the flow, if necessary. Some pumps have valves to adjust the flow, or you can restrict the flow by installing a separate valve on the outlet side of the pump or by using a special restriction clamp that attaches to the outlet tubing. (Never restrict the flow on the inlet side of the pump; also, do not restrict the flow on the outlet or discharge side by more than 25 percent.) A typical flow-control valve is shown on page 54. Before buying the pump, find out if the dealer will allow you to exchange it for a larger size if it turns out to be too small to operate the waterfall to your satisfaction.

Other Pump Considerations

After you've determined what size pump you need, you still have several other decisions to make about the type of pump you want.

Submersible or External? First, decide whether you want to use a submersible pump or an external (recirculating) pump. For most garden ponds, submersible pumps are a better way to go because they

run cooler and quieter than external pumps, and they are generally less expensive. In most cases, they're also more economical to install and operate because less plumbing is required. Reasonably priced models range from 180 gph to 1,200 gph; high-capacity models are at 3,400 gph. Most submersible pumps can be used in conjunction with mechanical or biological filters to produce clear water. These filters are discussed on page 65. The pumps themselves come with strainers or prefilters on the pump inlet to keep leaves and other debris from clogging the pump impeller. The only time you need to remove the pump from the pond is to clean the attached filter or strainer. Some submersible pumps come with flow-regulator valves; others don't.

Usually, external pumps, like those used for swimming pools, are practical only for very large waterfalls and fountains, or in situations where a submersible pump would be unsightly or impractical, such as in a pond that doubles as a wading pool. With capacities ranging from 2,400 gph to over 8,000 gph, and a maximum head of up to 80 feet, external pumps are overkill for most backyard ponds. If you're installing a swimming pool, though, you might consider plumbing the pump and filtration system to also operate a pond and waterfall. If a submersible pump doesn't work with your pond design, you can buy a pump designed to operate either in open air or submersed. Compact in size, they're a good compromise in situations where a submersed pump would be unsightly or prone to damage and typical external pump would be too big for the pond. For external operation, these pumps usually have to be placed in a dry sump below the water level of the pond. Capacities are similar to submersible pumps above.

Determining Quality. When selecting a pump, buy the best you can afford. The least expensive (and

least durable) pumps have plastic housings and components. Their output is limited to about 300 gph or less, and they have a relatively short life span. They are suitable for occasional operation of relatively small water features, and they are designed for submersible use only.

Most pumps used for ponds have cast-aluminum housings with a corrosion-resistant epoxy finish. They are more durable and impact-resistant than plastic pumps, they are moderately priced, and they come in a wide range of capacities. However, aluminum-housed pumps are designed for freshwater use only, since aluminum will quickly corrode in saltwater, chlorinated water, or water frequently treated with pond chemicals. Also, if you add fish to the pond, the water will be slightly acidic. This condition will eventually erode the aluminum housing and components of the pump. So, aluminum-housed pumps are not recommended for such situations.

The most durable (and most expensive) pumps use a combination of brass, bronze, and stainless-steel components and housings. These pumps will withstand a variety of water conditions, including salty and chlorinated water. They're rated for continuous operation and will outlast the other pumps mentioned. Usually, they come in larger sizes only (800 gph or higher). If you expect the pond to be a permanent feature in your yard, these pumps are well worth the extra initial cost. When selecting a pump, also consider energy efficiency. Compare the pump's amp rating (or wattage, if it is given) to the output in gallons per hour. If two pumps have the same output, the one with the lower amp rating will usually be more energy-efficient. If you plan to add a biological or mechanical filter to the system, find out if it can be fitted to the pump you've chosen. With some pumps, your choices of filters will be limited; other pumps are more versatile. For more on choosing and installing pond filters, see page 65.

When selecting a pump, make sure the cord is long enough to reach the proposed or existing electrical outlet. Many pumps come with a 6-foot cord, which won't work if local codes require the electrical outlet to be 6 or more feet away from the pond edge. However, you can usually order longer cords from the pump manufacturer as an option. Use only cords and plugs specifically designed for use with the pump. Do not use extension cords to increase the cord length. For more on wiring pumps, see page 9.

Waterfall Types

Waterfalls look best and are less prone to water loss when large, overhanging rocks are used for the lip of the falls. Use smooth, flat flagstones to produce a wide, thin curtain of water; or direct the water through a narrow gap between large boulders to produce a gushing effect. Creating a hollow space behind the falls will amplify and echo the sound of falling water. To avoid losing a lot of water, you can use rocks or masonry materials to build up the pond walls behind the lip and on both sides of the falls to direct any splashes back into the pond. The lips of formal waterfalls can be brick, tile, flagstone, or timbers. Some designs incorporate a clear sheet of acrylic plastic to create a wide, nearly transparent curtain of water. The plastic itself is all but invisible when the falls are in operation. The drawings show several options for natural and formal waterfalls.

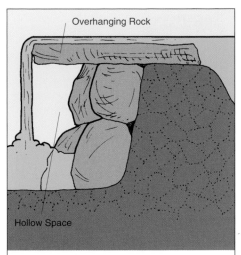

Waterfall Types. Flat, overhanging rock allows water to fall curtain-like, directly into the pond. Hollow space behind the falls echoes the sound of splashing water.

Clear Acrylic Plastic

Waterfall Types. A low weir (top left), a formal weir backed by clear acrylic plastic (bottom left), a narrow cascade (top right), and a wooden flume (bottom right) are just a few of the many possibilities for waterfalls.

Streams

We've all admired swift-flowing streams and rivulets in nature. But contrary to what you might think, the stream bed is not steeply sloped to produce this effect. Natural mountain streams usually arrange themselves into a series of short, fairly flat sections, separated by low falls or cascades. So, when building a stream between a series of falls, be sure to make the bed as level as possible along its length, so that it will retain some water when the pump is turned off. Alternating between wet and dry conditions can crack mortar or concrete, or shorten the life of the plastic or fiberglass liner materials. A stream with some water at all times will also look more realistic. A drop of 1 to 2 inches per 10 feet is all that is needed to make the stream flow downhill. Also make sure that the stream bed or catch basin is level across its width, and that the banks are roughly of equal height; otherwise, the watercourse will look lopsided.

Controlling Water Speed & Direction

To increase the speed of the current, bring the stream banks closer together; for a more leisurely current, move the banks farther apart. A deep, wide, slow-moving stream is preferable to a fast, narrow one if you want to grow shallow-water bog plants along the edges. However, you should avoid large areas of slow-moving shallow water, because they will soon become clogged with thick mats of algae. In either case, a meandering course will look more realistic than a straight channel. Vary the size of the rocks along the banks and the distance between the banks. Placing large rocks inside the watercourse will create rapids, and placing smaller stones and pebbles produce a rippling effect. Both of these make the stream look and sound more natural.

When placing rocks for the stream and waterfall, do not mortar the top layer of rocks in place until you have installed the pump and run water down the course. With the water running, experiment with the placement of stones of different sizes and shapes in the stream bed and along the banks. Producing the exact effect you want may take a bit of trial and error, so take your time. In some cases, you may need to build up the banks of the stream or basin behind the falls to prevent water from splashing outside the watercourse or overflowing the banks.

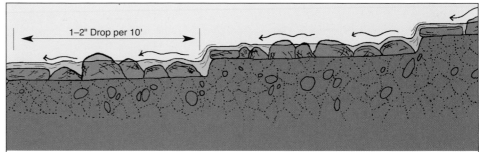

Streams. Dig the stream bed in a series of short, level sections between low waterfalls. Each section should hold some water when the pump is turned off.

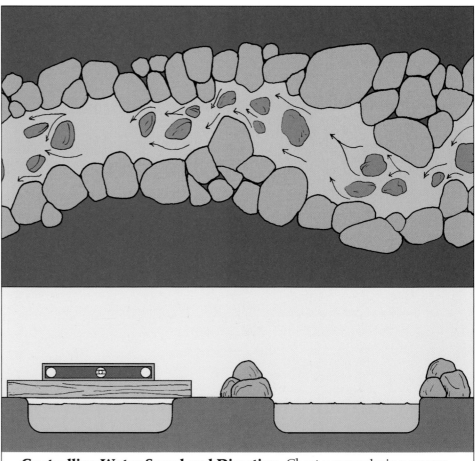

Controlling Water Speed and Direction. Chart a meandering course for the stream. Placing rocks in the stream bed will increase the current speed and make the stream look more natural (top). When digging the stream bed, make sure it is level across its width. Build up the banks with rocks to prevent splashing and overflow (bottom).

Lining the Watercourse

As with ponds, the stream beds and catch basins for waterfalls must be lined to prevent water loss. The same materials used to line ponds are also used to line the watercourse. The easiest to use and most versa-tile material is a flexible EPDM liner, although preformed rigid shells of plastic or fiberglass are also available. Don't line a watercourse with concrete or plastic cement, though, because the alternating wet and dry cycles will cause cracks. However, either cement or mortar is often used in conjunction with a flexible liner or preformed shell to hold large rocks in place along the watercourse and at the waterfall lip.

Flexible Liners

In waterfall construction, a flexible liner serves as a waterproof barrier under rocks, pebbles, and other decorative materials and directs any seepage back into the main pond. Flexible liners adapt well to both formal and informal waterfall designs.

Ideally, you should use one large piece of liner for both the waterfall and the main pond, to provide a continuous, seamless barrier. In practice, though, it is not always easy to align a square or rectangular sheet of liner material with the selected waterfall site without creating large amounts of waste material. More often, you'll have to figure the amount of material required by the pond and the waterfall separately. Usually, it is less expensive to order one large sheet, and then cut one or more strips from it to line the watercourse, rather than to order separate sheets for the watercourse and pond. You then glue or tape the sheets together where they overlap. (Special seam tapes and vinyl seam adhesives are available from the liner dealer for this purpose.) For more on sizing liners, see page 25. If the watercourse will be approximately the same width along its entire length, one long strip can be used. If the watercourse consists of pools and cascades of different lengths and widths, two or more separate pieces may be required. Allow sufficient overlap (at least 12 inches) at joints to prevent seepage due to capillary action.

Preformed Watercourses

Most companies that make rigid, preformed fiberglass or plastic ponds also offer preformed waterfall runs or courses made of the same material. These are installed much like a preformed rigid pond shell. (See page 34.) Informal preformed watercourses are shaped (and sometimes colored) to simulate natural rock, although most look fake unless the edges are disguised with over-hanging stones or other materials.

Preformed watercourses have one main advantage over flexible liners: The design has been worked out in advance. Formal preformed waterfalls are usually smaller versions of square or rectangular preformed ponds, with a built-in lip or spillway. The units are arranged in overlapping tiers to produce a symmetrical series of falls into the main pond. Fiberglass and plastic

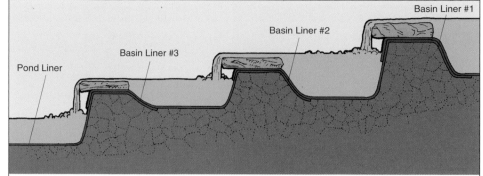

Flexible Liners. Flexible liner material can also be used for the watercourse. A continuous liner for the pond and waterfall is best, although pieces can be overlapped as shown here.

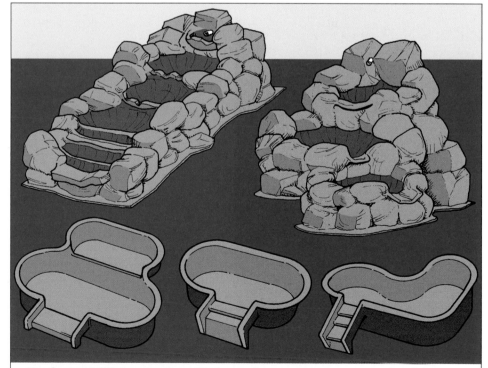

Preformed Watercourses. Preformed watercourses are made of the same rigid plastic or fiberglass material as preformed ponds.

water runs are lightweight and inexpensive; but, as with preformed ponds, the sizes and designs are limited. The premolded units consist of one or more small basins with built-in cascades and a lower lip that empties into the pond. You can combine two or more short watercourses in a series to produce a longer watercourse, each run emptying into the one below it. However, often you're still limited to the combinations recommended by the manufacturer, because each watercourse is designed to match the output of a particular-size pump: specifically from 200 to 500 gph for small units, and up to 1,300 gph for larger ones. If the pump is too small, the flow will be insufficient to achieve the desired effect; if the pump is too large, water will splash outside the watercourse or overflow the banks. (If you do oversize the pump, you can always divert some of the flow to operate another water feature or to run directly back into the pond.) Your supplier can help you choose a preformed watercourse to match the pump requirements of your pond. Preformed watercourses made of cement or reconstituted stone are also available. Although these are more substantial and natural-looking than plastic or fiberglass units, they are much heavier. As a result, the practical size of these units is limited to only a few square feet.

Installing a Preformed Watercourse

Preformed watercourses are installed much like the preformed pond shells discussed on page 34. The main difference is that you'll be recessing the watercourses into a slope or berm (mound) above the pond. Here is how to proceed.

1 **Grading the Site.** If you're working with a natural slope above the pond, all you need to do is excavate a pocket in which you place the watercourse. On flat ground, you'll have to build up a firm soil base to support the shell at the appropriate height above the pond. Use the soil from the pond excavation. The sides of the berm should slope gently away from the watercourse in all directions, with enough space to add rocks, plants, or other landscape materials to disguise the edges of the watercourse. Firmly tamp the built-up soil to provide support for the unit. Next, set the preformed watercourse in position on top of the mound; and mark its outline on the ground with flour, powdered gypsum, or a series of short stakes.

2 **Digging the Hole.** If you are installing more than one unit, start with the bottom one. Dig a hole to match the size and shape of the watercourse. If you're using a pre-

cast stone or concrete unit, tamp the soil firmly to prevent settling; then add a few shovel loads of wet cement in the bottom of the excavation to anchor the unit in place. Fiberglass and plastic units require firm support on the sides and bottom, or else they will deform when filled with water. Add or remove soil as necessary to conform to the shape of the shell. Also, before installing a watercourse, determine where the pump outlet tubing or pipe will go, and bury it in place a few inches beneath the soil. Some manufacturers suggest that you run the pipe or tubing in the same excavation, underneath the watercourse. Check the instructions that come with the unit.

3 **Placing the Watercourse.** Position the watercourse in the excavation so that the lip or spillway overlaps the pond edge. Check to make sure the basin or basins of the watercourse are level in all directions with a 4-foot level. If the level isn't long enough place a straight 2x4 across the rim and put the level on the 2x4. Backfill around the edges with sand or sifted soil, packing it firmly into the excavation and checking the level frequently. Build the backfilled soil to a height of 1 to 2 inches below the outside edge of the shell (flange), or as recommended by the manufacturer. Run the unburied length of pump outlet tubing

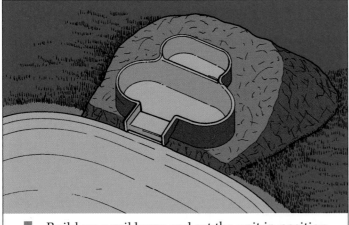

1 Build up a soil berm and set the unit in position. Mark the outline of a watercourse on the ground.

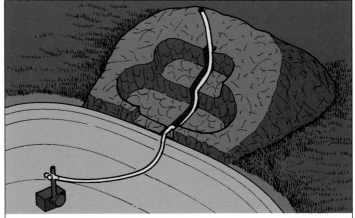

2 Excavate a hole to recess the unit into the side of the berm, or hill, above the pond. Run the pump outlet hose to the head of the watercourse.

into the top basin; secure it in place outside the watercourse with rocks, or as specified in the instructions.

4 Testing the Watercourse. Fill the watercourse with water, and check the water level around the rim to make sure the unit has remained level during the backfilling. If you haven't already done so, install the pump, attach the outlet tubing to it, and fill the main pond with water. Then pump water down the course. The water should flow evenly over the lip and any built-in cascades at a level of about 1 inch below the rim. (You should adjust the pump flow rate, if necessary.)

5 Placing Additional Units. If you will be installing additional sections of watercourse, follow steps 1 through 3 to install each successive one above the first. After installing and leveling each one, test it by running water down the course (step 4) and make any needed adjustments to the height and position of the unit. Make sure each unit is firmly positioned before installing the one above.

When all of the units are in place, connect the pump outlet pipe or tube to the top of the watercourse. Some units have built-in pipe or hose fittings for this purpose. With others, you can attach a short piece of plastic tubing to the outlet pipe; run the tubing over the rim at the top of the course; and disguise it with rocks or plants. Run the watercourse continuously for 48 hours; then recheck it for any settling, and readjust, if necessary.

6 Landscaping. Depending on the design of the unit, you may be able to use rocks or overhanging plants to disguise the edges of the watercourse and help blend it into the surrounding landscape. When setting large rocks or boulders around the rim, be careful that their weight does not crush or buckle the shell. For additional support, set the rocks or edging stones in a ribbon of concrete or cement mortar placed along the banks of the watercourse. If necessary, build up the edging above the surrounding ground level, and mortar between them to prevent soil from washing into the watercourse. Additional stones and ground-cover plants placed on the mound or surrounding slope will help prevent soil erosion.

3 Place the watercourse in the excavation and check that it is level. Backfill to hold the unit in place. Route the outlet tube into the top basin.

4 Turn on the pump and run water down the unit to make sure it works properly. Re-level the unit if necessary.

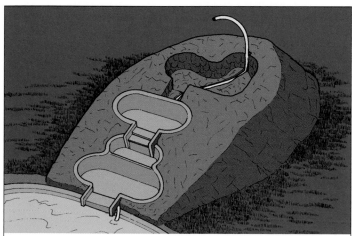

5 When installing multiple units, start with the bottom one; follow steps 1 to 4 to install each.

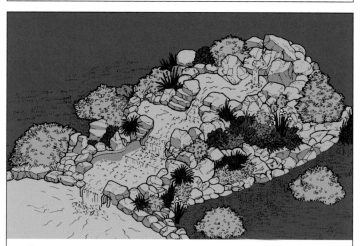

6 Place stones and plants around the unit to blend it into the landscape.

Installing a Lined Watercourse

If you're using a flexible plastic or rubber liner for your pond, excavate for the watercourse and install its liner at the same time. You can also add a lined watercourse to an existing pond of any material. Follow the instructions on page 24 for installing a vinyl-liner pond, along with the steps below for building the watercourse. When sizing the liner, allow enough extra material in the main pond to extend up and over the first waterfall lip and into the first catch basin.

1 **Grading the Site.** On flat ground, build up a berm of compacted soil next to the pond at the waterfall location. Make the berm large enough to accommodate the watercourse, with additional space around the perimeter to accommodate rocks and other landscaping materials. Where possible, slope the sides gently away from the proposed excavation to prevent runoff from washing dirt into the watercourse. Avoid steeply-sloped mounds, because they will be more prone to soil erosion. On sloping sites, cut level terraces into the hillside in which to dig the catch basins. Allow enough level space around each proposed hole to add rocks or other edging materials. For short lengths of stream, use a similar cut-and-fill procedure to provide a level course for the stream bed. On the ground, mark the location of the catch basins and connecting streams or cascades with stakes, flour, nontoxic spray paint, or a similar marking device.

2 **Excavating Catch Basins.** When you dig holes for the catch basins, remember that the finished watercourse will look smaller than the excavated holes once the rocks or other edging materials are in place. Because the catch basins are essentially mini-versions of the main pond, follow the same procedures outlined in steps 1 through

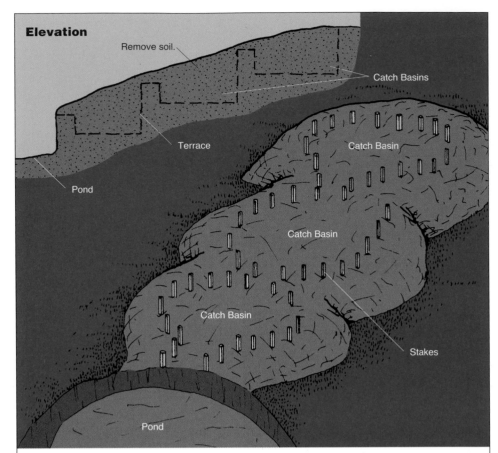

1 On a hillside site, cut level terraces into the hill at the waterfall location for catch basins. On flat sites, build up a soil berm and mark the basin locations with stakes.

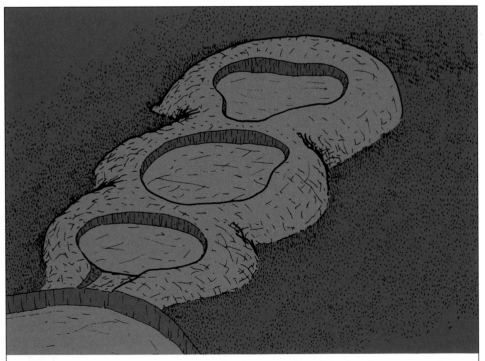

2 Excavate basins; make sure the bottom of each is level, not sloped.

7 on pages 25–28 to dig and level the basins. If the catch basin is large enough, you may want to cut a shallow ledge around the perimeter of the basin in which to set partially submerged boulders or other edging materials.

3 Excavating a Stream Bed.

Use a series of leveled strings as guides to dig the stream to the appropriate depth. The bottom of the stream bed should be level, or at a very slight slope toward the pond, so that some water will remain in the stream when the pump is turned off. Streams look most natural if they are made in a series of short, level sections connected by low waterfalls. Use stakes and string or a level placed on top of a 2x4 to level the stream bed across its width.

4 Supporting the Waterfall Lip.

Allow a minimum of 12 inches of compacted soil between each catch basin to provide a stable base for the waterfall lip. For a firmer base in loose or sandy soil, use masonry blocks, poured concrete, or rubble to separate the catch basins and to provide support for waterfall lip materials.

5 Positioning the Liners. Start

by fitting the liner for the main pond, allowing enough overlap at the waterfall end to extend up and over the first waterfall lip. If you're using a single liner for the pond and watercourse, drape the liner over the entire excavation. Slowly fill the pond with water to hold the liner in place, and allow it to settle into its final position. To protect the liner, place a piece of liner underlayment under the liner where it overlaps the waterfall lip. Cut and fit the next piece of liner in the lowest catch basin, providing sufficient overlap with the main pond liner. Overlap the liners for additional catch basins in the same manner. For additional protection against leaks, join each liner with a special seam adhesive or seam tape (available from the liner dealer).

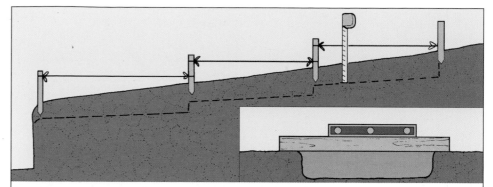

3 Excavate the stream bed by cutting a series of stepped, leveled trenches into the slope. A zigzag or wandering course looks most natural. Level the stream bed across its width.

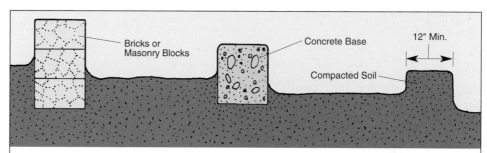

4 Reinforce waterfall lips by compacting soil or building a base of poured concrete, brick, or masonry blocks.

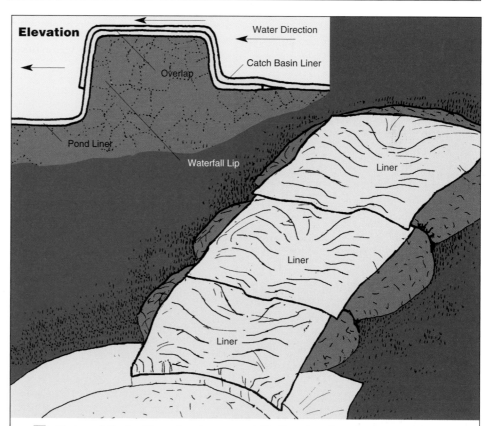

5 Cut and fit the liner for the waterfall. Overlap liner pieces at the waterfall lips, as shown. Adhesive or seam tape can be used to join pieces at overlaps.

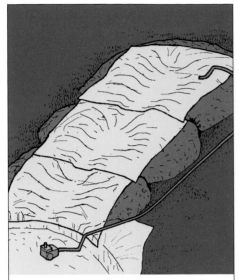

6 Install the pump and run outlet tubing or pipe alongside the watercourse to its top basin.

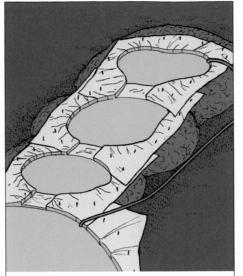

7 Fill catch basins with water, and use 20d nails or long spikes to hold the liner in position.

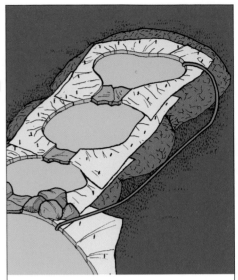

8 Position flat rocks or masonry units for waterfall lips. Build up large stones on either side of the lip to form channels.

6 **Installing the Pump.** Run the pipe or tubing alongside the watercourse from the point where it exits the pond to the top catch basin or head of the falls. (For more on installing pumps, see page 49.)

7 **Checking for Level.** After placing each liner, fill the catch basin(s) with water, as you did for the pond, to settle the liner in place. Check for leaks, and note the water level around the rim of each basin. If you note any high or low spots, remove or add soil beneath the liner, as necessary, to level the basin. To keep the liner in place while adding edging, push 20d nails through the liner into the ground every foot or so around the edges, above the waterline.

8 **Finishing the Waterfalls.** Start by positioning the overhanging rocks or other edging materials across the waterfall lip and on either side of it. For a more natural effect, you can also place stones behind the waterfall beneath the lip, to hide the liner. The top surface of the stones, or weir, should be just slightly below the water level of the stream or basin above, so that water will flow from one basin to the next without

overflowing the banks. Turn on the pump and notice how water flows over each weir; adjust the height and angle of the stones, if necessary, to provide a pleasing cascade. When you're satisfied with the results, place remaining stones around the perimeter of each basin or along the stream banks to hide the liner edges. Mortaring the rocks in place will prevent them from slipping into the watercourse. Additional stones may be placed in the watercourse to alter the flow pattern, although you should avoid using gravel in the stream bed because it will soon become clogged with algae and silt.

9 **Landscaping.** If you're building a natural-looking watercourse, arrange additional rocks and boulders of various sizes in the vicinity of the waterfall. Provide planting pockets between the stones for low shrubs, annuals, ground covers, succulents, and the like.

Use a combination of large boulders, medium-size rocks, and small pebbles to avoid making the waterfall area look like a man-made pile of rocks.

9 Finish landscaping the waterfall by placing rocks to hide liner edges. Turn on the pump, and run water down the falls to see how they work. Rocks placed in stream and basins will alter the course of water down the falls. Experiment with sizes and placement of rocks in falls to achieve a desired effect.

Installing the Pump

Follow the pump manufacturer's instructions for plumbing and wiring the pump. When you order the pump, also order all the required fittings, valves, and pipe needed to operate the waterfall. At the same time, order any other water features you may wish to include, such as a separate filter or fountain. As mentioned, you should order an electrical cord long enough to reach from the pump location to the electrical outlet. (For more on plumbing filters in the system, see page 39.)

Electrical Requirements

In many municipalities, a licensed electrician must do the wiring. In all cases, though, you should check local codes for outdoor electrical requirements before you start. Make sure all outlets, wiring, and connections are designed for outdoor use. Most small submersible pumps come with a waterproof cord, which you plug into a GFCI receptacle housed in a weatherproof outlet box. With some larger pumps (submersible and external), you wire the cord directly into the circuit, with the connection enclosed in a weather-proof junction box near the pond. The latter method requires a GFCI breaker wired into the circuit, either in the main panel or in a subpanel. In either case, it is a good idea to wire the circuit so you can control the pump by a switch located inside the house. If possible, locate the outlet or junction box in an inconspicuous and protected area, such as under a deck or against the side of a building. Unless the cable you're using is designed for underground use, encase it in PVC (grey) electrical conduit. In either case, bury the cable at least 18 inches deep so it won't be disturbed by spades, rototillers, or other gardening equipment. Again, check local codes for outdoor electrical requirements. (See Utility Access on page 9.)

Plumbing Requirements

Plumbing requirements will vary, depending on the pump model, length of the pipe run, and the number of water features the pump will operate. Some pumps are sold with a length of inexpensive clear plastic tubing, which is a larger-diameter version of the type used for aquarium pumps. Although such tubing is adequate for short runs, it has several drawbacks. First, the thin walls of the tubing are easily crushed or kinked, so you can't bury it underground or make it conform to sharp bends. If, on the other hand, the tubing is exposed to sunlight, algae will build up on the inner walls, restricting flow. Because exposure to sunlight will eventually make the tubing brittle, it must be replaced periodically.

One solution is to run a short piece of flexible tubing from the pump to the pond edge; then connect it to a rigid PVC pipe that runs to the top catch basin at the head of the falls. Or, you can use a higher-grade reinforced flexible tubing for the entire run, or a special black vinyl tubing sold by pump suppliers. Do not use garden hose, however.

When ordering tubing or pipe, the diameter must match or exceed the hose requirements for the pump. If you reduce the diameter, the pump flow will be restricted.

When you run the end of the outlet hose or pipe into the top of the water-course, you may find that the water pressure produces a strong jet that causes water to splash outside the catch basin. If this happens, run the hose under a small pile of rocks in the catch basin; or fit a short section of larger perforated pipe or hose over the end of the outlet.

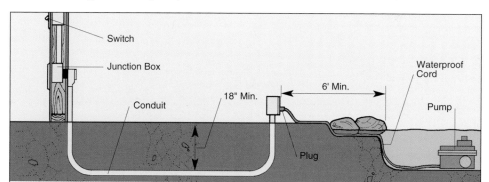

Electrical Requirements. Submersible pumps must be connected to a GFCI-protected circuit. Here, the circuit is wired so the pump can be operated from inside the house.

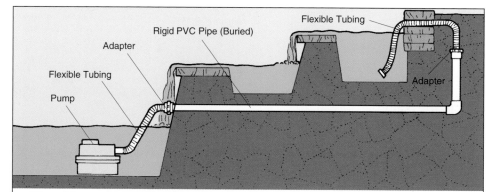

Plumbing Requirements. For long pipe runs, use rigid PVC pipe, buried in a trench alongside the waterfall. Connect the pump to the pipe with a short length of flexible tubing. This enables you to easily remove the pump from the pond for cleaning and maintenance. Secure all connections with hose clamps.

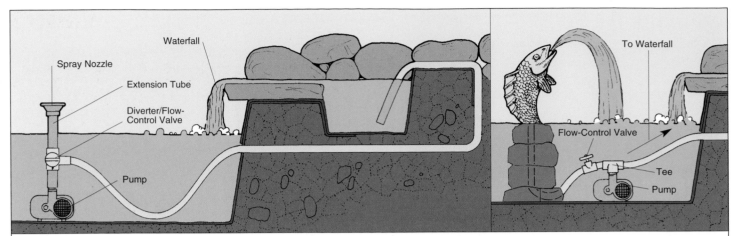

Fittings. Install a flow-control valve in the shorter of the two pipe runs to regulate flow to both features. As you restrict flow to one feature, the flow to the other feature increases (left). A diverter valve controls the flow to both the fountainhead and waterfall. Many spray fountain kits come with this feature (right).

Fittings. Pump suppliers offer a wide range of fittings and adaptors for their pumps to connect them to various water features. Your pump supplier can help you choose the appropriate fittings for your particular application. Most fittings for flexible plastic tubing are a barbed, push-fit type, whereas fittings and connections for rigid PVC pipe are either threaded or welded with PVC cement. When using push-type fittings, install hose clamps at all connections to prevent leaks. Some pumps require brass fittings on the pump discharge (volute), which may or may not include a flow-control valve. Depending on the pump design, you may need to install an adaptor fitting to convert to flexible tubing or rigid PVC pipe. Adding a tee fitting with a diverter valve enables you to operate two water features at once, such as a fountain and waterfall. You can accomplish the same result by installing an in-line flow-control valve in the shorter of the two pipe runs, as shown. Both types of fittings enable you to regulate the amount of water supplied to each feature. If you don't install a diverter or flow-control valve, the pumped water will take the path of least resistance (i.e., the shorter pipe run). The result will be either too little flow to operate one feature, or too much flow to operate the other, or both.

Keep in mind that the pump should have enough capacity to operate both features, pond and waterfall. When plumbing the waterfall, keep sharp bends and right-angle couplings to a minimum, as these tend to restrict flow. Use nontoxic plastic valves and fittings wherever possible; brass and other metal fittings can corrode and may be toxic to fish. Plastic ball valves have largely replaced old-fashioned metal gate valves in pond and swimming pool plumbing applications.

Float Valves. Another fixture you may find useful is a float valve used to top off the pool. Several different types are available. They work much like a ballcock valve in a toilet tank; when the water level drops, the float lowers, opening a valve that allows more water to be fed into the pond through a pipe or tubing connected to a nearby faucet. The system is separate from the pump plumbing. A simple setup using a bobby-float valve (like the ones used for evaporative coolers) is shown. Here, the valve is clamped to a short steel rod mortared between stones just below the waterline. The valve is connected to the main water supply by means of ¼-inch-diameter copper or plastic tubing. When installing such a system, make sure there is no chance of pond water siphoning back into the water supply. As usual, check the local codes about installation.

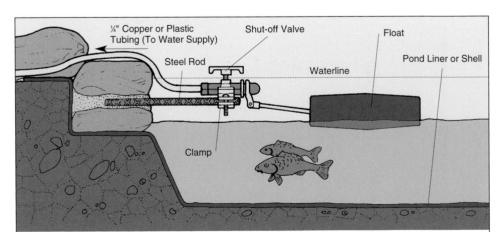

Float Valves. An inexpensive bobby-float valve attached to the pond edge will keep the water level constant. Similar devices are available at water-garden suppliers.

fountains

Types of Fountains

There are two basic kinds of fountains: sprays (or fountain jets) and ornamental statuary.

Sprays

A fountain spray consists of a jet nozzle or ring attached to the outlet pipe of the pump above the pond's water level. It produces an attractive ornamental spray. When run from the pump to a level just beneath the water surface, a fountain spray made from a length of vertical pipe will provide a natural-looking geyser effect. For a larger, more dramatic geyser, you should use a geyser jet fitting like the one shown. Because they introduce air bubbles into the spray, geyser jets are excellent for aerating the water, although they must be sized and placed carefully to avoid stirring up silt and sediment in the pond and producing cloudy water as a result. To be visually effective, geysers usually require large-capacity pumps. The drawing shows several popular fountain-spray patterns.

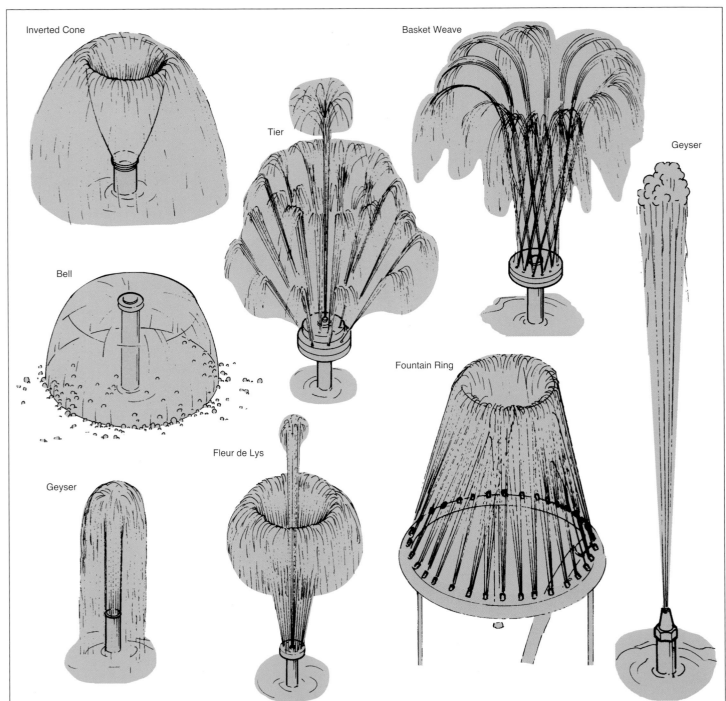

Sprays. Fountain Jets come in a wide variety of ornamental spray patterns. Shown here are some of the classics. Choose a pattern that fits the size, design, and mood of your pond.

Most jet nozzles are made of molded plastic and come with all the fittings required for installation. These include the correct-size pump and usually a flow-control valve that enables you to adjust the height of the spray. Higher-quality nozzles can be disassembled to make cleaning the jet holes easier; lesser-quality nozzles are more difficult to clean. Brass nozzles are generally used for larger water displays, but they're more expensive than plastic. Keep in mind that nozzles with small holes clog easily and will require frequent cleaning.

If you choose a spray-type fountain, place it in a sheltered area so that wind gusts don't disrupt the spray pattern or blow the water outside the fountain receptacle. Nozzles that produce delicate sprays or thin films of water (such as water-bell jets) need to be installed in a virtually wind-free location.

Statuary fountains

Statuary fountains run the gamut of designs from classical Greek figures and wall-mounted gargoyles to modern art forms and whimsical spouting frogs or fish. Most statuary fountains sold at garden and patio suppliers are precast concrete or cement. They come with a variety of colors and surface finishes to simulate other materials, such as stone, alabaster, or bronze. Some suppliers also carry modern sculpture fountains made of copper, brass, or bronze. Although on-site selections are usually limited, most suppliers can order what you want through catalogs. In times past, fountain statuary was often made of lead. If you find one of these relics, be warned that lead is toxic to fish and other aquatic life.

You can buy statuary fountain ornaments separately to put in the pond or next to it. Or you can buy these ornaments as complete, self-contained units with precast reservoir bowls and integrated pre-plumbed pump/filter systems. Precast pool pedestals of various heights are available for mounting statues or water jets in the pond. Fountain options are too numerous to describe in this book. Make sure, though, that you choose one that fits the style and size of your pond or garden. A large fountain can visually overwhelm a small pond and disrupt the water surface, making it difficult to raise water plants or to view fish beneath the surface. Also, if the spray is too large for the size of the pond, excessive water evaporation will be a problem.

Statuary fountains. Whether traditional or contemporary, ornamental statues lend a formal touch to the garden. Thumb through catalogs at your local patio supply or statuary dealer.

Installing a Fountain Spray

The way to install a spray nozzle depends largely on the pump you've chosen and the fittings available for it. Because so many variations exist, we cannot provide specific instructions for every situation. The easiest route is to buy a fountain spray kit, which includes your choice of spray nozzle, all required fittings, and a matched pump. Fittings are either press-fit or threaded, and they can be assembled in just a few minutes.

The outlet for most submersible pumps designed for fountains is located on the top of the pump. With this arrangement, the vertical rigid PVC discharge pipe can be attached directly to the outlet. (On some units, an adaptor fitting may be required.) You cut the pipe to extend the required distance above the water level (typically 4 to 6 inches); then you attach the spray nozzle, as shown. If the pump has a side discharge, you'll need to install an elbow fitting. If you're also operating another water feature, such as a waterfall or second fountain, install a diverter control valve in the pipe, as shown. To prevent the nozzles from clogging, attach a special pre-filter or filter screen to the pump inlet (this is available from the pump supplier). Or, you can buy units that combine the pump and filter in a single housing. The filter should be easily accessible for routine cleaning.

To install the fountain, attach the fittings and spray nozzle according to the manufacturer's instructions. Place the pump on a flat, level section of the pond bottom. Make sure the pump and discharge pipe are firmly supported so the pipe remains perfectly vertical after it is installed. If the unit has a tendency to tip or move out of position, place a few bricks around and on top of the pump to hold it in place. To provide the appropriate electrical connection for the pump, follow the guidelines on page 49.

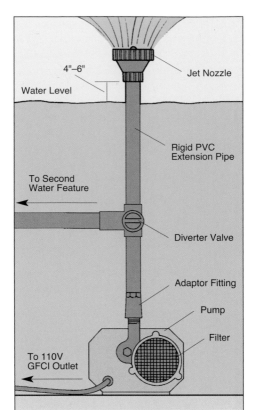

Installing a Fountain Spray. Jet nozzles can be attached directly to the pump outlet via extension pipes. Place the nozzle 4 to 6 in. above the water surface. You can plumb in a diverter valve to operate a second water feature (another fountain, waterfall, pond filter, etc.).

Underground Geyser

This simple water feature gives the illusion of a natural spring or geyser, welling up from the earth and returning to it. It is a good alternative if you don't want the hassle of maintaining a pond. As shown on the drawing, you create a lined, stone-filled "reservoir" in which you place the fountain assembly. The reservoir should hold about the same amount of water as the gallon capacity of the pump you've chosen. For a natural appearance, use a foaming geyser jet like the one shown. You could also use small bell sprays and single jets. Just make sure the spray does not extend past the edges of the reservoir. After installing the liner, place the assembly in the bottom of the reservoir. Then fit a large, inverted plastic plant basket (used for water plants) over the pump to keep gravel or rocks away from the pump inlet. Cut a small hole in the bottom of the basket, and slip it over the extension pipe; then install the jet nozzle. Next, fill the reservoir with clean, smooth creek stones, pebbles, or decorative rock about 2 to 4 inches in diameter. Weight down the edges of the liner with larger stones, or simply extend the rock fill as far beyond the edge of the reservoir as you want.

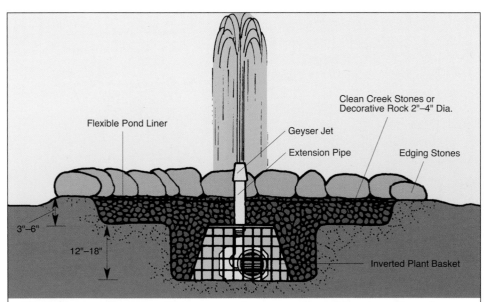

Underground geyser. Underground geysers fit well into small yard spaces; they make excellent water features if you don't want the hassle of maintaining a pond.

Installing a Statuary Fountain

Most statuary fountains come with a set of basic installation instructions. Use these in combination with the guidelines below to install the unit you've chosen.

A Self-Contained Fountain

In this type of fountain, a small submersible pump is typically housed in the statue pedestal, which sits in the reservoir bowl. The pump cord runs down an overflow tube inside the pedestal, through the bowl and hollow base. Most self-contained fountains have some way to access the pump for cleaning and maintenance. You should follow manufacturer's directions for assembly.

In-Pond Statuary

You can also place fountain statuary or ornaments inside the pond itself. The drawing below shows the basic setup. The statue itself has a supply pipe projecting from its base, which you connect to the pump with flexible tubing, as shown. You can mount the statue on a hollow in-pond

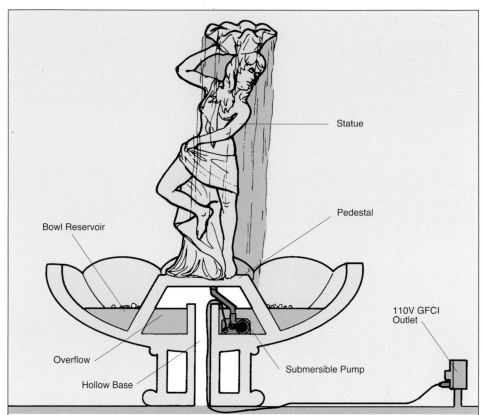

A Self-Containted Fountain. Self-contained fountains include pump and all fittings required to operate. A miniature submersible pump is hidden inside the hollow statue pedestal in the bowl reservoir.

pedestal, or build your own pedestal with mortared bricks, stones, or other masonry units. Some statuary fountains can be quite heavy, so you'll need to provide a firm base on the pond bottom.

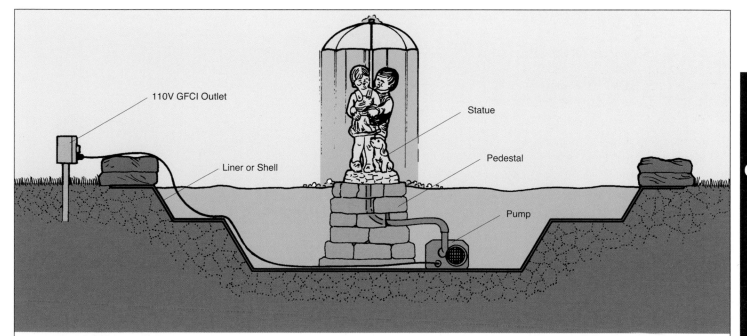

In-Pond Statuary. Statuary fountains can also be placed in ponds. Buy precast pedestal for this purpose, or build up a base of stone, brick, or other masonry units. Make the base hollow so you can connect the pump to the statue.

Installing the Fountain

1 Making A Footing. For heavy statues (over 100 pounds), provide a suitable footing underneath the pond shell or liner. This usually consists of a 4-inch-thick concrete subbase, a few inches wider and longer than the statue base, or pedestal. If you don't provide such a footing, the weight of the statue may tear the flexible pond liner or crack the rigid pond shell. Install the footing before you place the shell or liner. For lighter statues, all you need do is compact the soil firmly under the statue location before placing the shell or liner.

2 Installing the Pedestal. If you've purchased a statue pedestal, place it in the pond on top of the footing area. Otherwise, build up a pedestal with mortared bricks or stones. If you are using a flexible liner, cut a small piece of liner underlayment to place between the base of the pedestal and liner. Leave an opening near the bottom of the pedestal to run flexible tubing from the pump to the statue. To facilitate cleaning and maintenance, locate the pump outside the pedestal.

3 Installing the Pump. Situate the pump next to the pedestal. Run flexible tubing from the pump up through the pedestal, allowing enough extra tubing at the top to connect to the statue or ornament.

4 Installing the Statue. With a helper, move the statue in position on top of the pedestal. Tilt the statue slightly to make the connection between the pump outlet tubing and the pipe projecting from the statue base. (An adaptor fitting may be required.) Secure the connection with a hose clamp, and then rest the statue in its final position. It is not a good idea to mortar or otherwise affix the statue to the pedestal, in case you need to replace the outlet tubing at a later date.

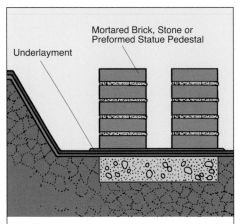

Pond Liner
Concrete Footing
Underlayment

1 When installing a flexible liner, provide a concrete footing underneath to support the weight of the statue.

Underlayment
Mortared Brick, Stone or Preformed Statue Pedestal

2 Build up the pedestal. Allow an opening near the pedestal base to run the pump outlet tubing. Underlayment protects the liner under the base.

4 With a helper, position the statue on the pedestal and connect outlet tubing to the fitting on the statue base.

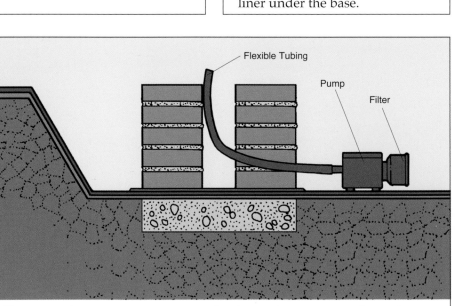

Flexible Tubing
Pump
Filter

3 Install the pump and filter; run flexible outlet tubing up through the base, allowing some extra at the top to facilitate the connection to the statue.

bridges

Wooden Bridges

A wooden bridge across a stream or a portion of a large pond provides architectural interest, as well as a shortcut from one side to the other. Bridges can be simple to ornate, depending on the style you've chosen for your pond and the various features around it. So, when designing a bridge, take the surrounding landscape into account. Also decide where the bridge will originate and end, and how

it will affect the location of paths and other landscape features in the yard. Size the bridge so that it is in proportion with the pond or stream. For a very narrow stream or small pond, a couple of wide planks laid from one bank to the other may suffice. Increase the width and height of the bridge accordingly for a larger body of water. Make the bridge wide enough to cross safely, yet in proportion with the pond and surrounding landscape. Bridges more than 12 to 18 inches

above the water should have handrails, both for safety and appearance. Bridges with spans longer than 8 feet will usually require vertical support posts set into the pond at midspan or every 6 to 8 feet. Be sure to provide a sturdy foundation for the support posts when you install the pond. The drawings show several simple bridge designs. Use pressure-treated or decay-resistant lumber, as well as rust-resistant hardware and fasteners, for all bridge members.

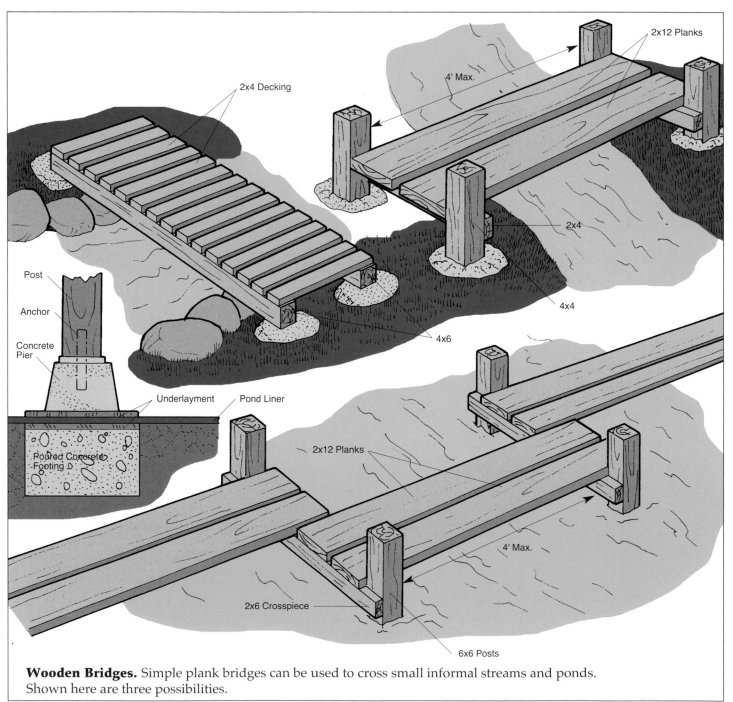

Wooden Bridges. Simple plank bridges can be used to cross small informal streams and ponds. Shown here are three possibilities.

Adding a Footbridge

A simple footbridge across your pond can be built with double 2x8s for support beams, 2x6s for decking and handrails, 4x4s for the posts, and ⅜-inch-diameter carriage bolts. The following describes a 5-foot-wide bridge to span a depression 6 feet across.

1. Positioning the Posts. Place two sets of three 4x4 posts on opposite sides of the depression. For a bridge with a railing, the posts should extend 4 feet above grade. If no railing is required, extend the posts about 1 foot above grade. You'll install two of the posts in each set 2 feet on center and the third 2 feet 6 inches on center. The two sets should be 7 feet apart on center for an 8-foot-long bridge. Lay three 8-foot-long double 2x8s across the depression as parallel and square as possible and as close as possible to their final position.

Measure and stake the locations of the posts, and then dig postholes to at least 6 inches below the frost line.

2. Installing the Posts. Set the 4x4 posts in a bed of gravel. Pour concrete an inch or so above grade at the support posts. Slope the concrete away from the posts for good drainage. The posts should reach above the planned top level of the 2x8 beams. You can trim the posts after the 2x8s

are in place. When the concrete sets, you are ready to lay the beams.

3. Installing Beams. Set the 2x8s against the outside support posts with the posts outside and to one side of the middle post. Check the beams for level with a carpenter's level. Make minor adjustments, and clamp them in place. When the 2x8s are level, nail them to the posts with 20d nails. Trim the posts off flush with the top of the beams (if you're not installing a handrail).

4. Securing Beams and Decking. With the 2x8s secured to the posts, drill two ⅜-inch holes through the posts and the beams where the posts meet the beams. Secure the beams to the posts with ⅜x7-inch carriage bolts.

Nail the 2x6 decking across the top of the beams; the 2x6s should overlap the beams 4¾ inches on each side. Keep the decking square by starting at either end of the beams with the first 2x6 flush with the ends of the beams. Space the 2x6s ¼ inch apart; use a spacer scrap to keep the distance equal. Nail the 2x6s to the beams with 10d nails.

5. Installing Handrails. If the codes require it, you'll have to install a handrail. Allow the 4x4 supports to run above the top of the beams by 3 feet or to the height specified by the local code. Attach a 2x4 or 2x6 handrail, edge side up. Handrails should be bolted with a minimum of two ⅜-inch-diameter carriage bolts at each post.

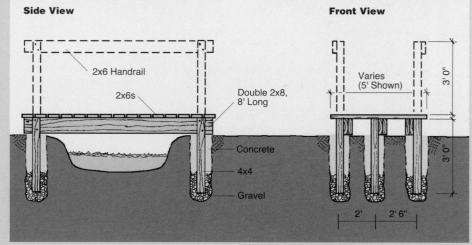

Side View
2x6 Handrail
2x6s
Double 2x8, 8' Long
Concrete
4x4
Gravel

Front View
Varies (5' Shown)
3' 0"
3' 0"
2'
2' 6"

Arched Bridge

If you would like a footbridge with a slight arch, cut the tops of 2x10s in an arc that drops from the full width at the center down to 7 inches at the ends. Handrails can be arched in the same manner. To lay out a smooth curve, tack nails into the board at the 7-inch mark at each end, and bend a ¼-inch-thick piece of wood against the nails up to the center edge of the board. Trace a cut line with a pencil. Make the cut with a portable saber saw, and sand the cuts with a belt sander for a smooth surface.

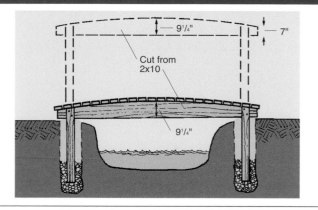

9¼"
7"
Cut from 2x10
9¼"

Stepping-stones

Stepping-stones are a convenient way to cross a pond or stream, but are not as visually obtrusive as a bridge. They can either lead all the way across the pond, or simply a few feet out into it for observing or feeding fish. For formal ponds, you can use square or rectangular cast-concrete stepping-stones or slabs, large quarry tiles, cut stone, or similar geometric masonry units. These are usually supported by piers of mortared bricks or concrete blocks. For informal ponds, you might use

irregularly shaped flat rocks or flag-stone, placed in a random pattern. If the pond is shallow enough, you may be able to use large rocks or stone slabs set directly in the pond. Otherwise, build up a layer of mortared flat rocks, or construct piers of poured concrete, brick, or block to support the stones.

If you've installed a flexible liner or preformed shell, you'll need to provide a suitable footing to support the stones and piers (if they are used). Protect the liner or shell by sandwiching it between layers of pond liner

underlayment, as shown. Stepping-stones usually look best if staggered in a zigzag or random pattern across the pond, rather than in a straight line. Place the stones close enough together so that people can walk without hopping, and make sure the stones are large enough to provide a stable footing. The surface of the stones should be high enough above the water so that they stay dry. Avoid placing the stones near a waterfall or fountain. Keep in mind that algae or moss will grow on wet surfaces, and make the stones slippery.

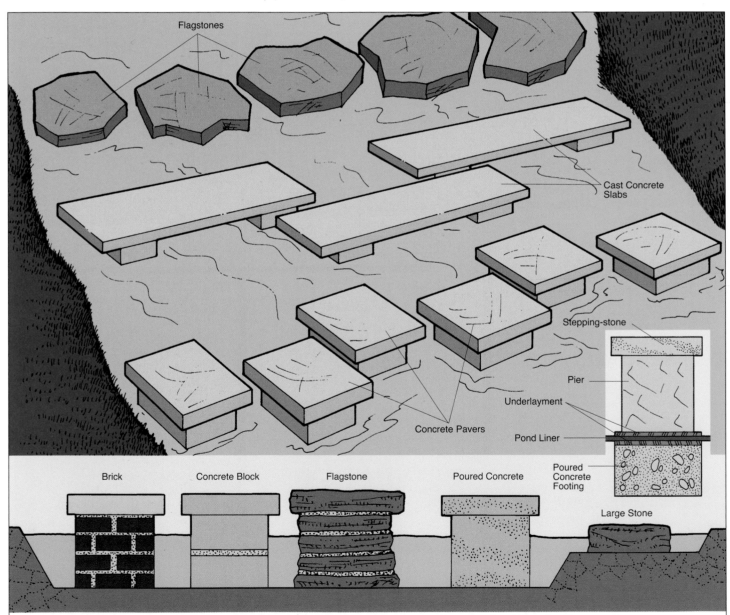

Stepping-stones. Stepping-stones look best if placed in a zigzag or staggered pattern. In deep water, construct piers to support the stones.

healthy water

Balancing the Water

The term "biological balance" simply means establishing a healthy ecological balance between plants, fish, and other aquatic life in the pond. Various factors affect ponds, including the size and depth, the amount of sunlight or shade, water temperature, water movement, pollutants in the water, and the kind and number of plants and fish. Depending on how these factors affect your pond, it may take anywhere from several weeks to several months to achieve this balance. Once the pond water is balanced, it will remain relatively clear provided you don't add fish, plants, or other pond life. Of course, if you do add any of these, you will need to take other measures to keep the water clear. Usually, you can do this just as you would with a swimming pool, by incorporating a mechanical or biological filter, using chemicals periodically, and routine cleaning.

How It Works

Think of your pond as a small, self-contained ecosystem. When you introduce aquatic plants, they draw nutrients (nitrates and phosphates) directly from the water and also the soil—if the plants are potted. These nutrients, combined with sunlight, cause the plants to grow and release oxygen into the water in a process known as photosynthesis. When fish are introduced, they consume the oxygen produced by the plants. To some measure, the fish rely on the plants as a source of food, and so keep excessive growth of the plants in check. In turn, the fish provide nutrients (carbon dioxide through breathing and nitrogen from fish wastes) to promote plant growth. Surface plants such as water lilies also benefit fish by providing shade during the hot summer months and controlling the water temperature. Plants give fish a place to hide from other fish, cats, raccoons, birds, and other predators. For their part, fish help control populations of plant-eating insects. Scavengers such as snails and tadpoles also help balance the pond by consuming excess fish food, algae, and organic debris. When the numbers of fish and plants in the pond are stabilized (not too many of one or the other), the pond is in biological balance.

The reason balanced ponds are relatively clear is because the plants and fish in tandem help control the algae growth that can turn the water cloudy.

Controlling Algae

When you first add water to your pond, it will be crystal clear. After a few days, however, the water will turn murky, taking on a greenish tinge. This is caused by microscopic single-celled free-floating algae. Unless you take measures to control these creatures, you'll end up with a thick pea soup of them.

It is normal for a pond to have excess algae growth until aquatic plants have established themselves. Submerged plants (oxygenating grasses) eventually starve out the algae by consuming available nutrients directly from the water. Surface plants like water lilies and

Balancing the Water. 1. Fish: Provide nutrients for plants (carbon dioxide, nitrogen); consume insect pests and some algae. **2.** Submerged plants (oxygenating grasses): Provide the highest level of oxygen of all plants; consume nutrients to control algae growth; and provide a dietary supplement and spawning area for fish. **3.** Scavengers (snails, tadpoles, pollywogs): Consume algae, decaying plant matter, and fish waste; provide nutrients for plants. **4.** Water lilies, floating plants: Provide oxygen and shade; leaves help prevent water evaporation; offer hiding places for larger fish to escape animal predators; consume nutrients to control algae growth. **5.** Marginal bog plants: Provide oxygen; consume nutrients to control algae growth; provide hiding places for small fish and snails; taller species shade pond edges in early morning, late afternoon.

various floating plants also consume nutrients, and they cut off the sunlight needed for algae to grow. The addition of fish and snails, and the eventual unplanned introduction of algae-eating insects like water fleas, also help to control algae, but to a lesser degree than plants.

You can always expect to have some algae in the pond, even after it is balanced. The slightly greenish tinge caused by floating algae is not harmful to fish or plants, and it helps conceal planters and the pump on the pond bottom. As the pond matures, most of the free-floating algae will eventually be replaced by various visible forms of hairy (filamentous), mossy, and slime algae growing on the sides and bottom of the pool, plants, rocks, and any other convenient surface. A small population of visible algae is actually beneficial, because it helps conceal the artifical-looking pond liner or shell. Like other plants, it also oxygenates the water. But when growth becomes excessive, it can choke out other plants and form unsightly mats of scum on the water surface. When such conditions exist, you'll need to physically remove the scum from the pond.

Adding a mechanical or biological filter to the system will help control both types of algae on a continuing basis, by trapping the algae cells and spores in the filtering medium. You can also use chemical algaecides for initial algae control after you first install the pond, and for periodic algae blooms afterwards. However, be careful in their use; some algaecides are toxic to fish, and most will affect the growth of other water plants. Consult your water-garden supplier or aquarium dealer for appropriate products and recommended dosages. Also, algaecides are just a temporary cure, killing existing algae in the pond. They do not guard against the growth of new algae, which is inevitable. If algae are a continuing problem, consult a pond specialist.

Starting the Process

To achieve an initial balance in a new pond, follow these procedures.

Testing the Water. When you first fill the pond with water, it may contain chemical and mineral pollutants that are toxic to fish and plants. The chemicals include chlorine, chlorine dioxide, chloramines, ammonia, and others present in tap water. Also included are various pollutants from pond-building materials, and poisonous chemicals that may have been washed or blown into the water from outside sources. Free chlorine in tap water usually dissipates after the water has stood for a few days. Other chemicals, such as a combination of chlorine and ammonia, take much longer to break down.

Before introducing plants or fish to the pond, test the water. After filling the pond, wait at least one week before testing. You can detect the presence of most toxic substances in water by testing for pH, ammonia, chloramines, nitrites, and water hardness. The pH is a measure of acidity or alkalinity. The scale ranges from 0 (highly acid) to 14 (highly alkaline), with 7 being neutral (indicating pure water). Healthy pond water ranges in pH from 6.5 to 8.5. Water-testing kits are available to test one or all of the conditions above. You can buy these kits at pet shops, garden suppliers, and pond dealers. Or you can order them from water-garden catalogs. The kit instructions usually tell you which water conditioners to use to correct the problem. Some pond dealers and pet shops also provide comprehensive water-testing services, and can advise you on proper treatment.

Correcting Water Conditions. A variety of water-conditioning treatments are available to balance the pH and remove toxic substances from ponds. But you should use them only if tests indicate that they are needed. Some fish and plant dealers recommend giving the pond a dose of a general-purpose water conditioner before adding fish or plants, just to be on the safe side. But if the water tests out all right, a conditioner isn't needed. If you do use one, follow the label directions. Even if you use a conditioner to achieve the initial water balance, you should still try to determine the source of pollution to prevent future problems.

In new ponds, lime leaching from concrete, cement, or mortar can cause severe alkaline conditions.

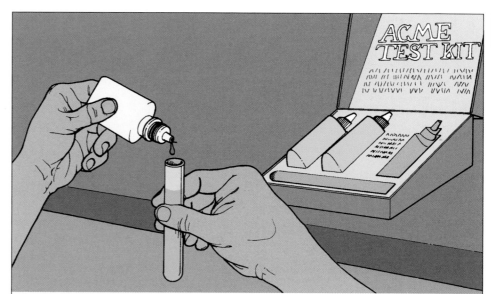

Testing the Water. Test water for pH and presence of chlorine, ammonia, and other toxic substances (see text). Simple test kits for monitoring water quality are available at pet shops and water-garden suppliers.

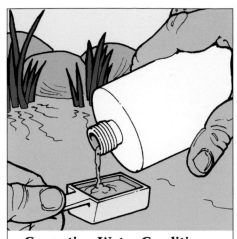

Correcting Water Conditions. If necessary, add a water conditioner to remove chlorine and other harmful chemicals in the water. Follow label directions.

Removing Algae and Plant Debris. If algae is present, treat water with algaecide. Remove leaves and other debris from the pond with a leaf skimmer.

will maintain depends on various environmental factors, including the amount of available oxygen, sunlight, and nutrients. A pond with good water circulation and filtration will support a larger population of fish than a stagnant pond with no filtration. A shaded pond may be healthier for fish, but will limit the types of water plants you can grow. It will take time and experimentation to find out what will grow in the pond and what won't, and to achieve a balance between plant and animal life.

For starters, use the following formulas for stocking your pond:

■ Two bunches of submerged plants (oxygenating grasses) per square yard of pond surface area.

■ One inch of goldfish or ½ inch of koi per 3 to 5 gallons of water, or 15 inches of fish per square yard (9 square feet) of pond surface area at a depth of 18 to 24 inches (three 5-inch fish, for example). Remember that small fish will grow into big fish.

■ One medium to large water lily for each square yard of surface area, or enough water lilies, lotus, or floating plants to cover 50 to 70 percent of

You can correct the problem by treating the concrete or mortar with a vinegar solution or commercial concrete curing agent, as described on pages 20 and 29. Metal pipes, pool paints, wood stains and preservatives, pipe-joint glues, and various other chemicals associated with pond materials can also poison fish and plants. Allow these to dry thoroughly before filling the pond with water. If you've already filled the pond and suspect pollution from these sources, drain the pond; clean all the surfaces and components thoroughly; and refill the pond with fresh water. (See page 74 for information on draining a pond.) If you suspect high concentrations of chemicals in the water supply, call the water company to find out what chemicals have been used, and how to neutralize them.

Removing Algae and Plant Debris. Even though it is not necessary to completely eliminate algae from the pond before introducing fish or plants, you can control any excess growth with the use of an algaecide. (See the precautions in Controlling Algae, on page 62.) If you have installed a filter, run it continuously for the first few days before introducing plants; clean mechanical filters daily. Also remove wind-blown leaves, blossoms, twigs, grass clippings, and

other debris from the pond daily with a leaf skimmer or pool net.

Introducing Fish and Plants. After filling the pond, wait several days to a week before introducing plants. Then, allow another two to three weeks for the plants to establish themselves (and to start the oxygenating process) before adding fish, snails, tadpoles, and other aquatic creatures. The size and number of plants and fish a pond

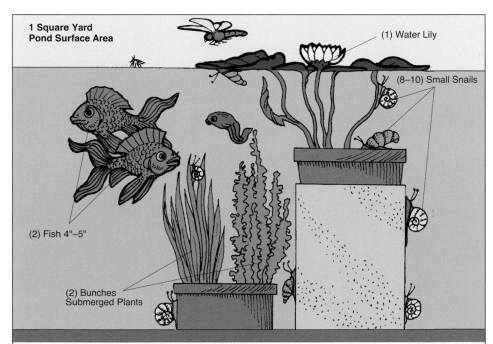

1 Square Yard Pond Surface Area

(1) Water Lily

(8–10) Small Snails

(2) Fish 4"–5"

(2) Bunches Submerged Plants

Introducing Fish and Plants. Add plants first; wait a few weeks for them to start the oxygenating cycle, and then add fish and snails. Use the ratio shown here for each square yard of pond surface area.

the pond surface during the summer months. Most water plants die back during the winter, and then re-establish themselves in spring. Once established, lilies and other water plants will occasionally need to be divided or pruned to prevent overcrowding.

■ Eight to ten small snails or six to eight large snails per square yard of pond surface area.

Filtration

The primary purpose of a filter is to trap suspended matter in the pond, including fish wastes, decaying organic matter, floating algae, leftover fish food, and other minute particles that cause cloudy water. Some types of filters also remove ammonia and other toxic chemicals. Although filters aren't essential to maintaining a healthy, balanced pond, they can help the process and dramatically increase water clarity. If your aim is to have a small ornamental pond with a few fish and plants, and you don't mind slightly cloudy water from time to time, you may not need a filter. If, on the other hand, you want crystal-clear water or you will be raising large numbers of fish, a good filter will certainly help. Koi ponds, particularly, require clear, relatively pure water, both for viewing the fish and to maintain their health. There are two basic types of filters: mechanical and biological.

Mechanical Filters

A wide variety of mechanical filters are available for ponds. Some are plumbed into the pump inlet (suction filters); others are plumbed to the pump outlet (pressure filters). Some go inside the pond; others, outside the pond. Most small ponds (under 1,000 gallons) employ an in-pond cartridge-type filter. These use a corrugated polyester filter medium, which looks much like an automobile oil filter and works in the same manner. Other small filters use small screens, foam, or woven fiber pads or wraps as filter media. Some

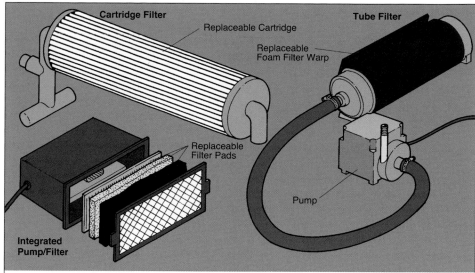

Mechanical Filters. Small mechanical filters are made especially for garden ponds. Several basic types are shown here (actual designs vary, depending on the manufacturer).

have provision for adding activated charcoal or a mineral called zeolite to remove ammonia and other chemical impurities from the water. None of these filter media has any particular advantage over another. The effectiveness of the filter depends more on the overall size of the filter (surface area of filter media in square feet and amount of water pumped through it in gph) than the type. Manufacturers generally provide performance specs for their filters, as for example, "for ponds up to 300 gallons."

For very large ponds (1,000 gallons or more), you can install a DE (diatomaceous earth) filter or a high-rate sand filter, like those used in swimming pools. These large filters must be placed outside the pond and require a large pump and extensive plumbing. Do not confuse mechanical filters with the filter screens and prefilters attached to pumps. The screens are meant to keep debris from clogging the pump impeller and fountain jets. (See page 40.)

To be effective, mechanical filters rely on a high flow rate. As a rule of thumb, you need a pump that can circulate the entire volume of pond water through the filter once every two hours (or as recommended by the manufacturer). Like pumps, filter

capacity is rated in gallons per hour. If you have installed a fountain or waterfall, you'll probably need a larger pump to provide sufficient circulation through the filter and still operate the fountain or waterfall. Your pump dealer can help you choose the right-size filter for your application. If your budget allows, select a filter that exceeds the minimum requirements for your pond. The larger the filter, the less often you'll have to clean it. The main drawback to mechanical filters is that they require frequent cleaning—at least once a week, and usually daily during the summer. Cleaning usually takes only a few minutes: You simply remove the filter pad, cartridge, or screen, and wash it off with a garden hose.

Biological Filters

These filters rely on beneficial bacteria (called nitrifiers) that feed on impurities in the water. The filter contains two or more layers of gravel or other media that harbor large concentrations of nitrifying bacteria naturally found in ponds. As water slowly flows through the media, the bacteria break down fish wastes and other organic matter. In the process, toxic ammonia created by fish waste and decaying organic matter are

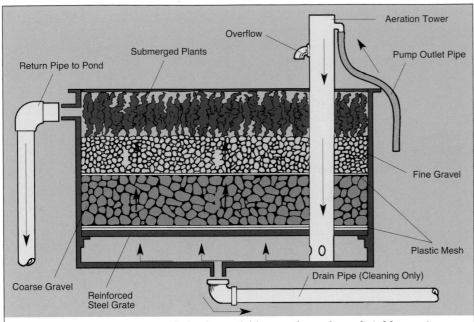

Biological Filters. Simple biological filters rely on beneficial bacteria, called nitrifiers, to remove wastes from the pond.

Labels in figure: Return Pipe to Pond; Submerged Plants; Overflow; Aeration Tower; Pump Outlet Pipe; Fine Gravel; Plastic Mesh; Drain Pipe (Cleaning Only); Coarse Gravel; Reinforced Steel Grate

transformed into harmless nitrates, which return to the pond to nourish plants. Other specialized microorganisims feast on single-celled algae passing through the filter. A simple biological filter is shown in the drawing. More complex types may incorporate mechanical prefilters or compartments filled with activated charcoal, zeolites, or other media. As shown, dirty water is pumped from the pond through an aeration tower to the bottom of the filter, where it slowly percolates up through the gravel filter media (giving the bacteria a chance to eat their fill!). It exits near the top of the filter by gravity flow through a return pipe to the pond. The aeration tower, combined with oxygenating grasses planted in the top layer of gravel, provides oxygen to help support the bacteria culture, as well as aquatic life in the pond. The layers of gravel also serve as a crude mechanical filter to trap suspended particulate in the water, further clarifying it. To clean the filter, all you need do is open a drain valve at the bottom to remove accumulated silt and sediment and lightly rinse the filter media to dislodge trapped particles. (Don't use heavy sprays of chlorinated tapwater, as this tends to

dislodge or even kill the beneficial bacteria in the filter media.)

Unlike mechanical filters, biological filters do not require a high flow rate to operate efficiently. (The pump need only turn over the total water volume every four to six hours.) Also, they need only be cleaned once every one to two months. On the downside, most biological filters are large, unsightly tanks located outside the pond above water level. So, you'll have to figure out a way to disguise the filter in the landscape (such as behind a shed or underneath a raised deck). Several manufacturers have recently introduced small in-pond biological filters, but their capacity is limited to ponds of 300 gallons or less.

When shopping for any type of filter, biological or mechanical, ask the advice of an independent dealer who carries several brands. Many filter manufacturers overrate the filtering ability of their products.

Other Filtering Devices

In addition to mechanical and biological filters, you can add other filtering devices to the system. Ultraviolet (UV) water sterilizers are sometimes used in conjunction with a biological filter.

Plumbed into the inlet side of the filter, these units consist of an ultraviolet bulb encased in a transparent, waterproof sleeve, which in turn is placed inside a tube plumbed into the system. When microscopic organisms are exposed to concentrated ultraviolet light, the UV energy causes the cell content (protoplasm) of the microorganisms to explode. Algae, bacteria, viruses, and certain fish parasites can be killed in this manner. The light also encourages minute organic particles to clump together so they can be trapped in the filter. The UV units are expensive, and usually they aren't needed if you have a good biological filter.

Ozone Generators. These devices sterilize water by reducing organic chemicals to their major elements of carbon dioxide and water. The generators convert oxygen in the air into ozone, and they infuse it into the water. The ozone effectively breaks down chloramines, ammonia, nitrates and phosphates into harmless gasses that escape the pond. Like UV sterilizers, ozone promotes the bonding of minute toxic waste particles so they are more easily trapped by the filter. Used for many years to sterilize water in swimming pools and spas, ozone generators are becoming popular for use in koi ponds because they remove nitrates from the water that otherwise must be consumed by plants. They're a good investment if you want a crystal-clear fish pond, with few or no plants in it.

Natural Plant Filters. This is another option for ponds with few or no plants. The filter is nothing more than a small pond or large tub filled with a thick growing bed of water plants, such as water hawthorne, watercress, shellflower, or water hyacinth, placed between the filter outlet and the main pond. Because the plants consume nitrates and other nutrients produced by the biological filter, they reduce algae growth in the main pond. They can also be made an attractive part of the landscape.

pond life

Aquatic Plants

When we think of aquatic plants, water lilies immediately come to mind. Water-gardening catalogs and pond books certainly give water lilies a good percentage of their space, and no water garden is complete without at least one of them. Nevertheless, many other water plants are suitable for garden ponds. Some, like submerged plants (oxygenating grasses), serve strictly utilitarian purposes; others have fascinating leaves or showy flowers. Most water gardeners want a good mixture of plants in and around the pond to create visual interest.

Water Lilies

Varieties of the water lily number in the hundreds, if not the thousands. But they are classified in two major groups, hardy and tropical.

Hardy lilies are frost-tolerant perennial plants. In temperate and cold climates, they die back to the roots during the cold season and re-emerge in the spring. In warm climates (not subject to heavy frosts), they stay in leaf all year around, although some species do poorly in tropical and subtropical environments. Most hardy lilies are characterized by blossoms that float on the water surface or rise slightly above it. Some varieties are fragrant; others have little or no fragrance.

Tropical lilies are frost-tender, which means they can be killed by repeated heavy frosts. Even though they can survive winters in tropical and subtropical zones (Southern Florida and Southern California, for example), they are treated as annual plants in most other parts of the country. To save them over the winter, you'll have to move the entire plant into a greenhouse. Tropicals are characterized by their strong fragrance and blossoms that stand well above the water level. If you want shades of blues and purples, you'll have to use tropicals, because hardy lilies don't come in these colors. Profuse bloomers, the tropicals produce four to five times as many blossoms as hardy lilies. They are also viviparous plants. This means they're capable of producing small plantlets on the leaf surface that can be removed and replanted. Tropicals can further be divided into day bloomers and night bloomers. The night bloomers open their blossoms at dusk, and they close in mid-morning to noon. You don't really need a flashlight to see them. With a few lights around the pond, you will be able to enjoy their striking nocturnal displays on warm summer evenings.

Both hardies and tropicals include some shade-tolerant varieties, which require only three or four hours of direct sunlight a day. But even these will do much better with more sun. Most other varieties require at least five or six hours of direct sunlight a day.

Because there are so many varieties, with more being developed each year, a comprehensive species list is beyond the scope of this book. However, we've included a few of the more popular varieties in the chart on page 78. Water garden catalogs will be your best bet for selecting lilies.

Planting Tips. Usually, lilies are first available from water gardens at the beginning of the growing season (once the danger of frost has passed). Instead of a plant with leaves and flowers, you'll get a piece of rootstock (called a rhizome for hardy lilies, or a tuber for tropical lilies), with a few emerging growing tips. Order as early as possible so the lily will have a chance to get established over the summer months.

Plant water lilies in wide, shallow containers, or special water lily bas-

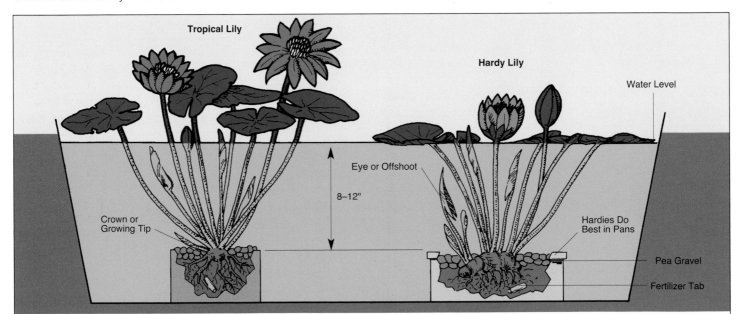

Water Lilies. Water lilies are by far the most popular pond plants. Hardy lilies grow as perennials in most climates; tropicals are treated as annuals in all but the warmest regions of the country.

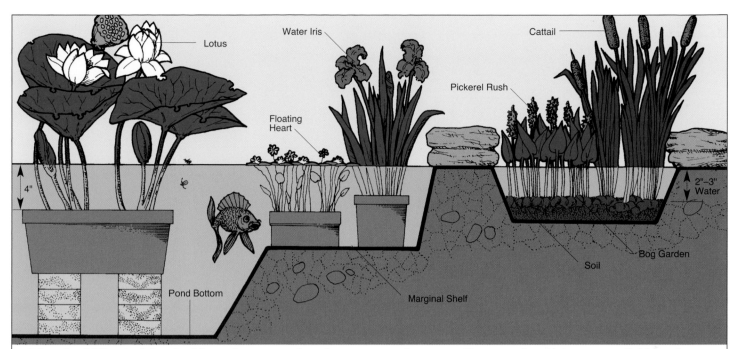

Marginal Plants. Marginal bog plants complete the water garden scene. Dozens of varieties are available; a few of the more popular species are shown here.

kets available from the water lily dealer. Allow plenty of room for growth. Add fertilizer tablets, if desired. Fill the container one-half full with heavy loam garden soil. If you are using plant baskets, line them with burlap to prevent soil from washing into the surrounding pond water. Avoid the use of organic mulches, peat moss, compost, commercial planting mixes, or ordinary garden fertilizers in your soil mix. Place the rootstock of hardy lilies horizontally, with the crown, or growing tips, near the edges of the container. For tropicals, place the rootstock vertically, in the center of the container. Fill the container with soil to a level just beneath the crown; then top it with a layer of pea gravel to hold the soil in place and to protect the roots from being uncovered or dislodged by larger fish. For tropicals, submerge the pot so that the crown or growing point on the lily is 6 to 12 inches below the water surface. With some hardies, the tips can be as much as 24 inches below the surface, although 6 to 18 inches is standard for most varieties. During the growing season, lightly spray the leaves with a garden hose every few days to dislodge aphids and other

harmful insects. (The plants and fish will thank you for this.) Special water-lily fertilizer tablets can be added each time you divide and repot the lilies, or once a year at the beginning of the growing season. For more specific growing instructions, refer to a water-gardening catalog.

Marginal Plants

A wide variety of shallow water plants is suitable for growing around the edges of the pond or in a separate bog garden. Marginal plants also do well in container gardens. Most marginal plants do best in rich soil topped with 2 to 3 inches of water, although some of the larger ones will grow in water up to 12 inches deep. Common marginal plants include lotus, floating heart, water iris, water hawthorne, cattail species, horsetail, sagittaria, pickerel rush, water clover, creeping jenny, taro, umbrella palm, water canna, and a wide variety of ornamental aquatic grasses. As with water lilies, there are tropical and hardy marginal plants. Consult a local nursery or water-garden supplier for plants that do well in your area.

Planting Tips. Planting techniques vary, depending on the species, and

there are many of them. The key is not to let the soil dry out! (Keep an eye on the water level, especially during the summer months.) Planting in pots will help confine the root system, and you can take frost-tender plants indoors for the winter. Put the pot in a larger, waterproof container, and fill it with water to keep the soil constantly wet. Select an indoor location that receives direct sunlight. To plant in the pond or bog garden, do the following:

First, gently hose off plants to remove any foreign matter, and keep the plant wet while planting. Fill the planting container (if one is used) with soil; then add a fertilizer tablet, as for water lilies on page 68. If the plant has a rhizome, trim and plant it horizontally with the growing tips just above the soil surface. Plants with tubers should be planted vertically. For all plants, tamp the soil firmly around the roots and cover them with ½ inch of washed pea gravel. Saturate the soil with water; then plant at the correct depth in the pond or bog garden. You can consult the plant dealer for more specific planting instructions and growing tips for the plants you've chosen.

Submerged Plants

As the name implies, submerged plants grow entirely underwater. Once you've planted them, you may not even be able to see them. Even so, they play an extremely important role in the pond ecology, as mentioned in the previous chapter. Also referred to as oxygenating grasses, they include some of the same species grown in aquariums, with the fernlike anacharis being the most common. Other submerged plants include cabomba (also called fanwort), with fan-shaped lacy leaves; myriophyllum, with fine, hair-like foliage (a favorite of spawning fish); and vallisneria (ribbon grass), with long, ribbonlike leaves.

Planting Tips. Plant in soil-filled pots to prevent excessive spreading. Add a thin layer of coarse gravel to keep soil in place and to help anchor the plant. (If the roots become dislodged, the plants will float to the surface.) Plants will grow in up to 30 inches of water, but they will do best if the topmost leaves are submerged to a depth of 6 to 12 inches beneath the water surface. Make sure the entire plant is well submerged. To keep fish from overgrazing the plants (fish are especially fond of anacharis), make a protective cover of lightweight plastic ½-inch mesh (bird netting). Wrap the mesh around the plant container, allowing 8 to 10 inches of material to extend above the container rim. Close the sides and top with twist ties to prevent fish from getting trapped inside. If you have enough fish in the pond, they'll keep the plants neatly pruned.

Floating Plants

These plants have buoyant leaves to keep them afloat, with roots dangling in the water beneath and requiring no soil. Floating plants such as water lettuce (also called shellflower), water fern, and duckweed are grown for their attractive or interesting foliage. This foliage provides shade for fish and helps control the algae growth. Some varieties, such as water poppy and water hyacinth, also produce showy flowers during the summer.

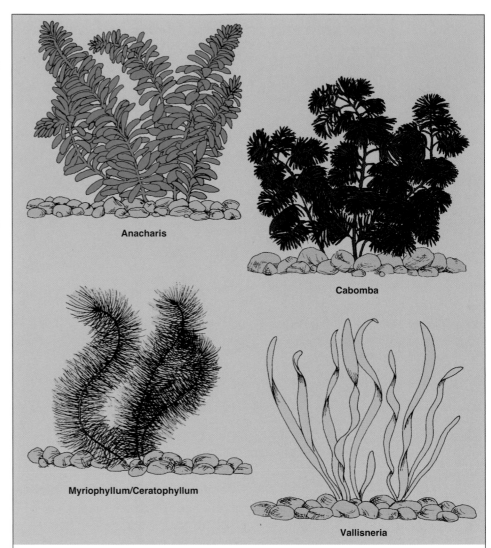

Anacharis

Cabomba

Myriophyllum/Ceratophyllum

Vallisneria

Submerged Plants. Submerged plants are essential to a balanced pond. Their main function is to oxygenate the water. They also provide food and hiding places for fish.

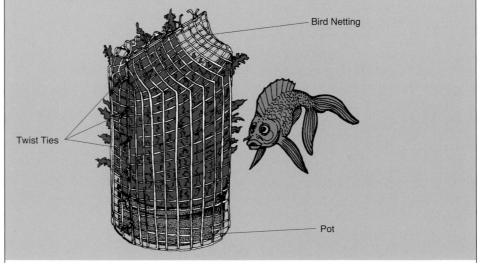

Bird Netting

Twist Ties

Pot

Planting Tips. Place netting over submerged plants to keep fish from overgrazing them.

Planting Tips. Like submerged plants, floating plants are sold by the bunch. Once you set them afloat in the pond, they require no particular care. These plants are considered hardy in warm climates; but they are treated as annuals in colder climates, where they're killed by winter frosts. The main drawback to floating plants is that they're highly invasive. During the summer months, they can quickly spread over the entire surface of a small pond, and occasionally they must be thinned out to keep their numbers in check. In warmer climates, they're considered a pest because they grow year-round, clogging natural waterways. For this reason, interstate shipments are forbidden in some of the southern states and in California.

Fish & Other Water Creatures

No water garden is complete without a few fish and water snails. Goldfish are the all-time favorites, although the Japanese koi is becoming increasingly popular as a playful water garden "pet." Other creatures, like tadpoles and salamanders, capture the interest of young and old alike. This section discusses these and other popular pond denizens.

Goldfish

Members of the carp family, goldfish are surprisingly hardy. They can withstand a wide range of climates and water conditions. Under favorable conditions, they breed readily in outdoor ponds. If you've ever visited a pet store (and who hasn't?), you know that in addition to common varieties (comets, moors, and fantails), you can also find fancier varieties. Stick with the common varieties in the beginning, since these usually tend to be hardier and can withstand a wider fluctuation in water temperature. Also, make sure the fish you choose are pond goldfish, which have been raised in outdoor conditions. For best results, choose healthy fish between 3 and 6 inches long. Avoid fish with

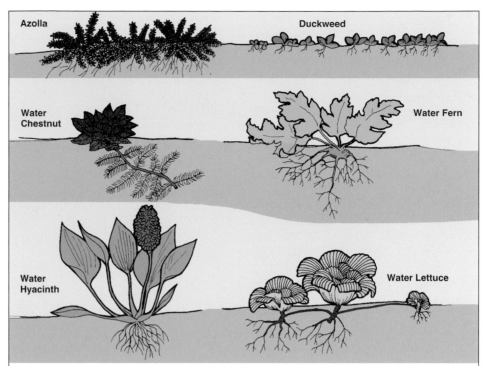

Floating Plants. Free-floating plants can be purchased in bunches and require no maintenance once you set them afloat. However, you may have to thin them out to keep them from taking over the pond.

drooping or tattered fins, dull or cloudy colors, or bumps and bruises on their bodies. If one or more of the fish in the tank looks sick, avoid the whole tank, because the other fish may also be infected.

Koi

Japanese koi (which means brocaded carp) are a close relative of the goldfish, but they are easily distinguished from goldfish by the short whiskers around their mouths. Colors include silvers, metallic gold, bright oranges, whites, lemon yellows, and various tricolor combinations. As with goldfish, koi have been bred to produce many named varieties (Kohaku, Asagi, Shusui, Koromo, and so on). Under ideal conditions, these colorful fish will grow up to 4 feet long and live well over 100 years. However, their average life expectancy in a garden pond is about 15 to 20 years, and they will grow to only about 2 feet long.

Koi are easily trained to eat from your hand and do simple tricks, like jumping through hoops or sucking from a

baby bottle. They'll often follow their owners around the edge of the pond, waiting for a handout. Koi owners insist that each fish has its own distinctive personality.

Koi and goldfish live quite happily together in the same pond, but water requirements for koi are more exacting. Because of their large size, they require a pond depth of about 30 to 36 inches, although more shallow areas can be incorporated for better viewing of the fish. The banks should be steep, and at least 18 inches above water level, so the fish don't jump out of the pond. In colder climates, koi usually won't survive the winter unless they are taken indoors. Breeding koi is a specialized hobby beyond the scope of this book, but several good books have been written on the subject.

Mosquito Fish

A humble relative of the fancy guppies sold in pet shops, mosquito fish (Gambusia affinis) are native to natural ponds, lakes, and watercourses throughout the warmer areas of the country. They're often introduced into man-made ponds or lakes to control the larvae of mosquitos and other pesky insects. Resembling a small minnow, mosquito fish grow to about 1 inch long. These hardy little fish reproduce rapidly under a variety of water conditions, although their numbers are generally kept in check by the size of the pond and the available food supply.

Mosquito fish require no special care; they feed on small insects, insect larvae, and leftover bits of goldfish food. They're generally too small (and too quick) to be bothered by animal predators. Larger fish, such as koi and goldfish, may eat mosquito fish, but generally they prefer other food.

Mosquito fish are not nearly as interesting or attractive as goldfish or koi. But they can play an equally important role in maintaining biological balance in a water garden. At the same time, they will also significantly reduce the numbers of pesky mosquitos. In some areas, you can obtain these little fish free or at a minimal charge from a local mosquito abatement agency, a city parks department, or a county agricultural extension office. Or, you can get an aquarium net and bucket, and try your luck at a nearby lake, pond, or reservoir.

Game Fish

For various reasons, catfish, trout, crappie, bluegill, bass, and other game fish usually don't do well in garden ponds. The main reason is that small, shallow bodies of water don't meet their temperature and oxygen requirements. Most game fish have adapted to relatively consistent temperatures found in larger, deeper bodies of water. Game fish are also aggressive by nature, and they will often pick on smaller fish or even eat them whole.

Amphibians

Frogs, newts, salamanders, and turtles are all likely candidates for the pond. Often, these creatures come to

Fish and Other Water Creatures. Many types of aquatic life can be introduced to a garden pond. Some will visit on their own accord.

the pond uninvited, especially in rural areas. Besides being good pond scavengers, tadpoles and pollywogs are fun to watch as they grow legs and transform into frogs. Newts go through a similar aquatic pollywog stage, characterized by their feathery external gills. Frogs, turtles, salamanders, and newts are likely to visit the pond to lay their eggs, but they're equally apt to travel some distance from the pond to forage for food. And keep in mind that if you overstock the pond with tadpoles, you may end up with a backyard full of croaking frogs!

Other Water Creatures

As mentioned, water snails help keep the pond clean by consuming algae and fish waste. They also serve to maintain the ecological balance of the pond. They're best known as nature's "vacuum cleaners", removing algae from the stems and leaves of larger water plants. (They won't eat the plants themselves.) Numerous varieties exist, but the black Japanese snail (Viviparus malleatus) is the most

popular. Water snails can be purchased at any aquarium shop. Also, when you buy your water plants, you're more than likely to get a few of these tiny hitchhikers (or their eggs). But don't worry—they won't crawl out of the pond and eat your garden plants!

Freshwater clams and mussels serve much the same purpose as snails, although they're somewhat more reclusive. Clams bury themselves in underwater plant containers or in the muck at the bottom of the pond. Mussels attach themselves to submerged rocks and other underwater surfaces. Freshwater mussels are particularly useful for filtering out floating algae, to help keep the water clear. Bear in mind that snails, clams, and mussels won't remove all the algae from your pond, no matter how many you have. And they should not be considered substitutes for a good filtration system and other more effective forms of algae control mentioned in this chapter.

maintenance

Pond Care

Maintaining a clean, healthy pond is like a cross between keeping up a garden and caring for an aquarium. Even during the summer months, when your pond requires the most attention, it shouldn't take you more than an hour or two every week to keep it in good shape.

Maintaining Water Quality

During the warm season, ponds lose water through evaporation, so you'll need to replace the water regularly. By doing so, you may introduce chemicals from the tap that can concentrate in the pond. These, combined with toxins produced by fish wastes and decaying plant matter, may eventually pollute the water and even disrupt the biological balance. This rarely happens in ponds with a good balance of plants and fish and adequate filtration systems. But it is possible, especially if you haven't been cleaning the filter regularly or the pond becomes overcrowded with fish and plants.

Ponds may also become polluted by runoff containing pesticides, herbicides, or other toxic chemicals.

For these reasons, periodically test the water (about once a month during the warm season), using a test kit as described on page 63. If the pond becomes polluted, correct the situation by partially draining it and adding fresh water. As a rule of thumb, you can replace up to 20 percent of the total water volume without affecting the biological balance of the pond. You should also test the water if your fish are showing signs of stress (gasping for air at the surface, swimming sideways or erratically, or acting lethargic). These conditions may also be symptoms of a biological disease, or simply a lack of oxygen in the water, which can happen during hot weather. If oxygen is the problem, partially drain the pond and refill it with fresh water. Run the pump continuously for a week or so; add more oxygenating plants, if necessary. If you suspect disease, though, consult your aquarium dealer for proper treatment.

Draining & Cleaning the Pond

If the water is severely polluted, choked with algae, or filled with sediment, you may have to completely drain the pond, clean it, and refill it with fresh water. Draining may also be necessary to find and repair a leak in the pond liner or shell. The best time to clean the pond is in late summer or early autumn. Plants are nearing the end of the growing season then, so you're less likely to stress them or to damage new shoots. Fish will also be less stressed at this time, and any fish that hatched in the spring should be big enough for you to net and remove from the pond. (If you clean the pond in the spring, you can disrupt spawning fish and amphibians, or damage the eggs.) Before you start, fill one or more holding tubs with some of the pond water. Drain the pond to within about 6 inches of the bottom; then carefully net out the fish and put them in the holding tank. (If you have a lot of fish, a kid's plastic wading pool or 50-gallon plastic trash can

Sump Pump · Small Wading Pool · Air Bubbler · Air Stone · Aquarium Pump · Leak-Proof Containers for Plants · Garden Hose · Plastic Dust Pan · Plastic Brush · Wet Newspaper · Fish Net

Draining and Cleaning the Pond. Shown is a basic collection of tools and materials needed to drain and clean a pond.

works well.) Add a few bunches of oxygenating plants to the tank, and place it in a shaded location. Allow about 1 gallon of water for each inch of fish. If the fish will be out of the pond for more than a few hours, place an aquarium air bubbler in the tank to provide additional oxygen.

Depending on the location of the pond, you can either siphon the water out with a garden hose that leads to a lower area in the yard, or you can pump the water out. Garden-hose adaptors are available for many pond pumps. If it's not possible to use the pond pump to remove the water (or it would simply take too long), you can rent a high-capacity sump pump at a tool rental shop. Run the pumped water into a nearby garden area; the nutrients in the water will benefit your plants. Don't allow the pump to run dry, though. Bail out any remaining water with a plastic bucket. Then remove the plants and place them in water-filled plastic buckets. If you have many large plants, like water lilies, wrap them in wet newspapers or burlap sacks; put them in a shady location; and spray them occasionally with a garden hose to keep them moist. When the pond is drained, sift through the silt and pick out as many snails as you can find. (You probably won't get them all.) Put these snails in the holding tank with the fish. Use a plastic dustpan to shovel out the silt on the pond bottom. Clean the sides and bottom with a stiff plastic brush or a strong jet from a garden hose. Do not use chemical cleaners—just water. As you work, be careful not to tear or puncture the liner or pond shell. Rinse and drain the pond several times to remove any remaining muck. Refill the pond with fresh water, and add a dechlorinating agent or water purifier, according to the manufacturer's instructions. Also pour a few buckets of the original pond water back into the pond to help re-establish the biological balance. Don't put the fish back into the pond until the water temperature returns to within 5 degrees of the temperature in the holding tank. As

with new ponds, you can expect increased algae growth until the ecological balance is reestablished.

Routine Maintenance

As in nature, garden ponds and their inhabitants go through seasonal cycles. With each season, you'll have a slightly different list of pond chores to perform.

Spring. In the spring, you may notice excessive algae blooms before lilies and other water plants have emerged to provide shade and consume nutrients. This problem will usually take care of itself once the aquatic plants have leafed out. Late spring is the time to introduce new aquatic plants, remove any dead foliage from existing ones, and clean out any debris in the pond that collected over the winter. After the last frost, you can divide, replant, and fertilize bog plants and water lilies. In cold climates, fish will still be lethargic and weak from winter hibernation, but they will begin to feed as the weather warms up. Now is the time to supplement their diet with easily digestible foods in small amounts (consult your aquarium dealer). Do not overfeed: The rule of thumb is to give the fish no

more food than they can eat within 10 minutes. Fish are also particularly susceptible to diseases at this time, so keep a close eye on them. In mid- to late spring, many fish and amphibians will spawn and produce eggs. To assist the process, you can place spawning mats (available from mail-order water-garden suppliers) in the pond. If you haven't been running the pump over the winter, inspect the pump, filter, plumbing, and electrical connections for damage. Have the pump cleaned and serviced by a reputable dealer, if necessary.

Summer. Pond activity reaches its height during the summer months. Aquatic plants will be growing rapidly and sending forth their colorful blooms. Spend a few minutes each day snipping off faded blossoms and keeping plants trimmed. Insects will start to appear, so keep an eye on plants. Avoid the use of insecticides in or near the pond. Hand-pick caterpillars and other pests from plants, and toss them in the pond for your fish. Use a hose to spray lily aphids from the water lily leaves.

As the weather becomes hotter, water evaporation will increase, so you'll have to "top off" the pond

Routine Maintenance. Throughout the growing season, clip dead leaves and fading blossoms from aquatic plants to keep the pond looking neat and tidy.

Summer. Do not use insecticides in or around the pond. Hand-pick insects or wash them off the plant leaves with a garden hose.

remove sick fish from the pond, and treat them with the appropriate fish medicine. Refer to a fish book or consult a local aquarium dealer for advice on choosing the correct treatment. Because pond life of all types flourishes during the summer, you'll need to clean the pump strainer and filter more frequently. As the water heats up, oxygen levels will drop, so it's a good idea to run the pump continuously.

Autumn. This season brings falling leaves, which must be removed from the pond every day before they have a chance to decay and pollute the water. If the pond is located near or under a tree, stretch netting over the pond to catch the leaves. Any leaves that do sink to the bottom of the pond can be removed with a soft plastic rake, pool sweep, or spa vacuum (available at water-garden suppliers). Pool sweeps and vacuums are also good for removing excess silt from the pond bottom. Be careful not to disturb rooted plants in the pond.

Clean the pump filter frequently. Continue pruning yellowed foliage from water plants. Fish may become hungrier as they build up stores of fat to survive the winter.

Winter. When the water temperature drops below 45 degrees Fahrenheit,

fish become inactive and stop eating. You don't need to feed them until the following spring, when they become active again. In warmer climates, fish may be fed all year around, or as long as they remain active. When ice forms on the pond, it can cut off oxygen to the fish, and trap toxic gasses beneath the surface. If the pond is frozen for more than a few days, the fish may suffocate. In mild climates, where ice is a temporary condition, you can place a pot of boiling water on the ice to melt a hole in it, as shown. In moderately cold climates, placing a circulating pump on the pond bottom (where the water is warmer) and directing the flow upward will prevent ice from forming in the middle of the pond. In extremely cold climates, use a floating pond de-icer to keep a hole open in the ice all winter. If you won't be running the pump during the winter, remove it from the pond and drain all pipes to keep them from cracking. To avoid damage to a biological filter, drain and rinse it. Allow it to dry out for the winter. When you put the filter back in service the following spring, it will take several weeks for the beneficial bacteria to reestablish themselves in the filter media. Move frost-tender plants indoors for the winter.

every day or two in order to keep the water level up. It's best to add a little water each day, rather than a large amount once a week.

As water temperatures rise, fish become susceptible to various diseases caused by bacteria, fungi, and parasites. So, inspect the fish frequently for signs of illness, which could include blotchy or discolored skin, missing scales, or lethargic/erratic movement. Immediately

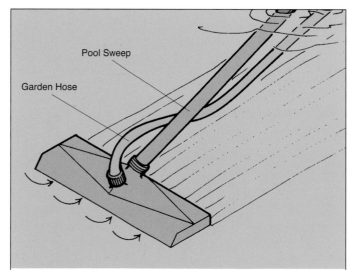

Autumn. Operating by water pressure from a garden hose, a pool sweep removes silt and sediment from the pond bottom.

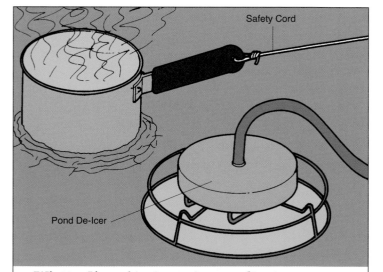

Winter. If pond ice is rare in your climate, use a pan of boiling water to melt a hole in the ice. In severe-winter climates, a floating pond de-icer keeps the hole open throughout winter.

Repairing a Pond Liner

Punctures and tears in flexible liners can be repaired with patching kits available from water-garden catalogs or the source where you bought the liner. The kits usually contain a small can of adhesive and a piece of liner for making patches. Tears in butyl rubber liners can also be repaired with a special laminate tape.

1 Completely drain the pond and locate the source of the leak. Make sure the tear or puncture is completely dry and clean. Before making the repair, find out what caused the tear or puncture (sharp rock, root, etc.) and remove it. Cushion the area behind the tear with damp sand or a piece of liner underlayment.

2 Cut a patch from the same material as the liner (butyl rubber or PVC plastic), about 2 inches wider and longer than the tear. Apply a thin, even coat of adhesive over the torn area, slightly larger than the patch.

3 Apply a coat of adhesive to the patch, making sure you cover the entire area. Allow the adhesive to become slightly tacky (about 2 to 3 minutes, or as recommended on the label directions).

4 Firmly press the patch in position, and smooth it to remove any wrinkles. Allow the adhesive to dry thoroughly before filling the pond with water.

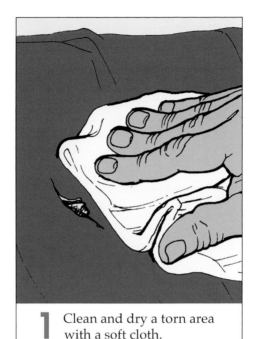

1 Clean and dry a torn area with a soft cloth.

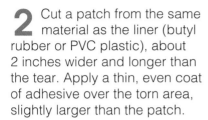

Patch

2 Apply adhesive to a torn area.

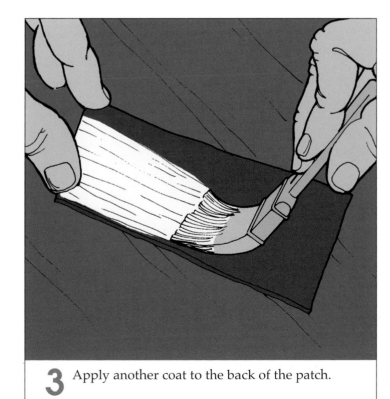

3 Apply another coat to the back of the patch.

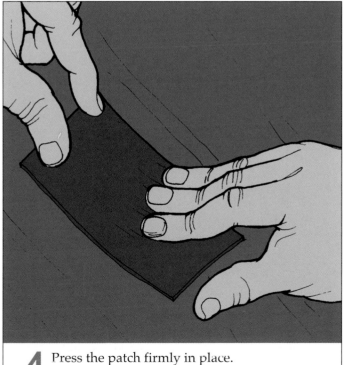

4 Press the patch firmly in place.

Hardy Water Lilies

Name	Description	Comments
Charlene Strawn	Clear, fragrant, medium-yellow blossoms with darker-yellow centers. Holds blossoms higher above water than most hardies. Plant has medium spread (6 to12 square feet), is shade-tolerant (3 hours minimum sun per day).	Prolific bloomer with long blooming season. Easy to propagate, good for beginners.
Marliac Carnea (also called Marliacea Carnea in some catalogs)	Very pale pink, slightly fragrant flowers about 3 to 5 inches across. Small to medium spread (1 to 8 square feet) Slightly shade-tolerant (4 hours minimum sun per day).	Vigorous plant, prolific bloomer. One of first hardies to break dormancy in spring.
Pink Beauty (formerly Fabiola)	Clear, medium-pink blossoms that bloom in clusters of two or three at a time. Slight fragrance. Plant has small spread (1 to 6 square feet), requires full sun (6 hours minimum sun per day).	Prolific bloomer, with long blooming season. Compact plant size makes it excellent for smaller ponds.
Splendida	Strawberry-red flowers with slight fragrance; medium spread (6 to 12 square feet). Shade-tolerant (4 hours minimum sun per day).	Good, medium-sized plant for pond of any size.
Virginia	Large, nearly double, white flowers with yellow centers. No fragrance, long blooming season. Shade-tolerant (4 hours minimum sun per day).	Very showy flowers, reaching about 9 inches across. Although it tolerates partial sun, it performs best with full sun.

Tropical Water Lilies

Name	Description	Comments
Dauben (also called Daubeniana)	Light, lavender-blue to white, minature flowers (about 2 to 4 inches across). Highly fragrant blooms, small spread (1 to 3 square feet) when planted in containers. Tolerates some shade (4 hours minimum sun per day). Day bloomer.	Prolific bloomer; often has several flowers at once. Compact size makes it an excellent choice for tub gardens and small ponds.
Margaret Mary	Pale to medium blue, fragrant blooms, medium spread (6 to 12 square feet). Tolerates some shade (4 hours minimum sun per day). Day bloomer, slightly viviparous.	While medium in size, plant will adapt to a 3.5-quart container.
Panama Pacific	Description: Bluish blossoms that deepen to a rich purple, with bright yellow centers. Slightly shade-tolerant (4 to 5 hours minimum sun per day). Small to large spread, depending on container size. Day bloomer, quite vivaparous.	Good, medium-sized plant for pond of any size.
Red Flare	Spectacular dark-red petals with deep maroon stamens, and red-tinged foliage. Medium to large spread (6 to 12+ square feet). Requires full sun (6 hours minimum sun per day). Night bloomer.	Exceptionally striking red flowers. Good for medium- to large-sized ponds.
Texas Shell Pink	Very large, pale-pink blossoms, prolific bloomer. Medium to large spread (6 to 12 square feet). Slightly shade-tolerant (4 to 5 hours minimum sun per day). Night bloomer.	Good for medium- to large-sized pools. Giant, light-colored blossoms show up well at night in dark ponds.
Wood's White Knight	Large, pure-white flowers with yellow stamens; prolific bloomer. Fragrant blooms, medium to large spread (6 to 12+ square feet). Shade-tolerant (3 to 4 hours minimum sun per day). Night bloomer.	Good for medium- to large-size ponds. Very prolific bloomer, with clusters of three or more large flowers borne at one time.

glossary

Acrylonitrile butadiene styrene (ABS) A plastic formulation (typically black in color) used for some rigid pond shells, also for drainpipe in plumbing systems.

Aeration The infusion of oxygen into water by mixing it with air, usually by means of a fountain spray or underwater air bubbler (such as those used in aquariums).

Algaecide A chemical treatment that prevents or controls algae growth.

Backfill Earth, sand, or gravel used to fill the excavated space under a pond shell or liner.

Balanced water Water with the correct ratio of mineral content and pH level that prevents an alkaline or acidic buildup.

Catch basin In a man-made stream or watercourse, a small depression or basin beneath a waterfall designed to hold water when the pump is turned off.

Chicken wire Flexible wire mesh used to reinforce thin concrete structures; also referred to as poultry netting. Sold in hardware stores, lumberyards, and home centers.

Chloramines Complex compounds formed when chlorine (from tapwater) combines with nitrates present in pond water. Toxic to fish and plant life, chloramines are difficult to neutralize by chemical means— the pond water usually must be partially or fully replaced to reduce chloramine levels.

Conduit Metal or plastic pipe used to encase buried or exposed electrical cables and protect them from moisture or physical damage.

Coping Stones, bricks, or other individual masonry units used as a finished edging around the pond perimeter. Coping can be set loose or mortared in place.

Crown The growing tip of a root system, from which a plant sprouts; the point at which plant stems meet the roots.

Dry well A gravel-filled hole used to receive and drain water runoff; part of a drainage system to which water runoff is directed via a perforated drainpipe.

Ethylene propylene diene monomer (EPDM) A kind of synthetic rubber. Flexible sheets of EPDM are used for pond liners. EPDM has greater stretch and UV resistance than PVC.

Footing The widened, below-ground portion of a poured-concrete foundation or foundation wall.

Frost heave Shifting or upheaval of the ground due to alternate freezing and thawing of water in the soil.

Frost line The maximum depth to which soil freezes in winter; your local building department can provide information on the frost line depth in your area.

Game fish Large, usually carnivorous fish such as trout, bass, pike and catfish. Due to specific oxygen, space, and temperature requirements, game fish don't do well in small garden ponds.

Grade The ground level. "On grade" means at or on the natural grade level.

Ground-fault circuit interrupter (GFCI) A safety circuit breaker that compares the amount of current entering a receptacle with the amount leaving. If there is a discrepancy, the GFCI breaks the circuit in 1/40 of a second. The device is usually required by code in outdoor areas that are subject to dampness.

Head The vertical distance between a pump and water outlet, used to determine pump performance. Pumps are sized by how much water (in gallons per hour) they can deliver at different "head" heights above the water level of the pond.

Light well A lighting fixture recessed below ground level that directs light upward, typically used to highlight tall plantings or other features beside the pond.

Marginal plants Various plant species that grow in wet or boggy soil around the edges of a stream or pond; also called Bog Plants.

Mil One one-thousandth of an inch; the measurement used to gauge the thickness of PVC and rubber pond liners.

Nitrifiers Beneficial bacteria present in pond water that break down fish wastes and other organic matter, transforming toxic ammonia into harmless nitrates, which nourish plants.

Oxygenating grasses Various species of submerged plants used primarily to add oxygen to pond water.

pH A measure of acidity or alkalinity of soil or water. The pH scale ranges from 0 (acid) to 14 (alkaline). Midpoint 7 represents neutral (neither acid or alkaline). Healthy pond water ranges in pH from 6.5 to 8.5.

Photosynthesis The synthesis of carbohydrates by plants from carbon dioxide, water, and inorganic nutrients (nitrates and phosphates) using sunlight as an energy source with the aid of plant chlorophyll.

Pier A concrete or masonry block rising above ground level to support the structure above it.

Plastic cement A dry cement mixture that includes a powdered latex additive to reduce cracking and serves as a waterproofing agent.

Polyvinyl chloride (PVC) A type of plastic formulation. Thin, flexible sheets of PVC plastic are used for pond liners. Rigid PVC plastic pipe is used for water supply lines.

Reinforcement bar Often called Rebar. Steel rods used to reinforce thick concrete structures to prevent cracking.

Rhizome A spreading underground stem or runner, which forms the root stock for hardy water lilies and some other water plants.

Runoff Water traveling across the ground surface, caused by heavy rains or irrigation. If the surrounding ground is sloped toward a pond, surface runoff can wash dirt and garden chemicals into a pond.

Scavengers In garden ponds, creatures such as snails, mussels, clams, or tadpoles that feed on fish wastes, algae, and dead organic matter.

Sod Sections of turf or grass cut from a lawn (usually with a flat-blade shovel) that contain both the root system and topgrowth. Can be replanted if kept moist.

Swale A broad, shallow ditch or depression in the ground, either occurring naturally, or excavated for the purpose of directing water runoff.

Topography The relief features or surface configuration of an area; the contour of the land.

Tuber The enlarged fleshy portion of an underground stem or rhizome; a potato is one example. Tropical lilies are tuberous plants.

Ultraviolet light (UV) Invisible rays at the extreme violet end of the sun's light spectrum, which causes color fading and deterioration of certain materials, such as plastics. Most pond liners have chemical additives to inhibit the effects of UV rays.

Underlayment A thick fabric material placed under a flexible pond liner to protect it from sharp stones or other sharp objects in the pond excavation. Get underlayment materials from pond dealers.

Variance A formal waiver from a municipal building department or similar agency to allow an exception to local codes or ordinances on a nonconforming feature of a building project.

Weir A notched obstruction or spillway placed across a stream to create a waterfall.

index

- Access to pond, planning, 8, 12
  Acidity, water, 63
  Algae, controlling, 62-64
  Alkalinity, correcting, 63-64
  Amphibians, 72
  Anacharis, 70
  Azolla, 71
- Balancing pond water, 62-64
  Biological balance, 62
  Biological filters, 65-66
  Bobby valve, 50
  Bog gardens, 12, 69
  Bridges, 13, 58-59
- Cabomba, 70
  Capacity, pond, 21-22
     calculating, 22
  Cattail, 69
  Chlorine, removing, 63
  Cleaning pond, 74-76
  Codes, local, 22
  Concrete ponds, 20, 29
  Conduit, electrical, 49
  Copings: see Edgings
  Creeping jenny, 69
- Decks, 13
  De-icer for pond, 76
  Depth, pond, 21
  Draining pond, 74-75
  Duckweed, 70-71
- EPDM (rubber pond liner), 12, 18, 43
  Edgings, 12-13, 28, 36
  Electrical requirements, pumps, 9, 49
  Excavation, 26, 34, 44
     flexible liner pond, 26
     performed shell, 34
     watercourses, 44, 46-47
- Fiberglass pond shells, 19
  Filters, 65-66
     biological, 65-66
     mechanical, 65
  Fish, 64, 71-72, 76
     diseases, 76
     types, 71-72
  Fish net, 74
  Flagstones, 60
  Float valve, 50
  Floating plants, 70-71
  Flow control valve, 50
  Flume, 41
  Formal pond styles, 10-11
  Fountains, 52-56
     geysers, 54
     sprays, 52, 54
     statuary, 53, 55-56
  Frogs, 72
- Game fish, 72
  Ground-fault circuit interrupter
     (GFCI), 9, 49
  Goldfish, 71

  Grading for watercourse, 46
- Head, pump, 39
  Hillside lots, pond installation, 8-9, 46
  Horsetail, 69
  House, proximity of pond to, 6
- Ice, removing, 76
  Informal pond styles, 11-12
- Kits, pond, 21
  Kits, water testing, 63
  Koi, Japanese, 21, 71
- Leveling pond, 27
  Lighting, pond, 9, 14-15
  Lime, leaching, 63-64
  Lotus, 69
- Maintenance, pond, 74-76
  Marginal plants, 12, 69
  Mechanical filters, 65
  Mosquito fish, 71-72
  Myriophyllum, 70
- Newts, 72
- Oxygenating grasses, 62-64
  Ozone generators, 66
- Paths, 12
  pH, 63
  Pickerel rush, 69
  Piers, 60
  Planning ponds, 6-16
  Plant debris, removing, 64, 76
  Plantings, locating, 16
  Plants, aquatic, 64, 66, 68-71
     as filters, 66
     bog, 69
     floating, 70-71
     oxygenating grasses, 62-64, 70
     submerged, 70
     water lilies, 64, 68, 78
  Plumbing requirements, 49-50
  Pollywogs, 62, 64, 72
  Polyvinyl Chloride (PVC), 18, 49
  Pond liners, flexible, 18-19, 24-32
     installing, 25-32
     raised pond, 30-32
     repairing, 77
     sizing, 24-25
     underlayment for, 19
  Pond shells, preformed, 19, 34-36
     choosing, 19
     installing, 34-36
     raised pond, 36
  Pool sweep, 76
  Property lines, marking, 15
  Pumps, 38-41
     choosing, 38-39
     filters for, 65-66
     installing, 49-50
     positioning, 39
- Raised pond, building, 30-32, 36
  Reinforcement bar (Rebar), 20
  Rubber pond liners (EPDM), 12, 18, 43

- Safety tips, 4
  Sagittaria, 69
  Salamanders, 72
  Scavengers, 62, 64, 72
  Seating, pondside, 12
  Shade, effect on ponds, 6-7
  Shade screens, 7
  Shelves, plants, 26
  Site plans, drawings, 15-16
  Site selection, 6-9
  Snails, water, 62, 64, 72
  Sod, removing, 25
  Soil conditions, 8-9
  Sprays, fountains, 52-54
  Statuary fountains, 53, 55-56
  Submerged plants, 70
  Sump pump, 74
  Stepping-stones, 13, 60
  Streams, 42, see also Waterfalls
  Styles, pond, 10-12
     formal, 10-11
     informal, 11-12
  Submersible pumps, 40
  Sun, effect on pond, 6-8
  Surrounds, pond, 12
- Tadpoles, 62, 64, 72
  Testing water, 63
  Topography, 8-9
  Trees, as wind control, 7
  Tub gardens, 21
  Tube filters, 65
  Turtles, 72
- Ultraviolet water sterilizers, 66
  Umbrella palm, 69
  Underwater lights, 14-15
  Utility access, 9
- Vallisneria, 70
- Water conditioners, 63-64
  Water lilies, 64, 68-69, 78
     planting tips, 68-69
     species list, 78
  Water plants, 68-71
  Water quality, 62-66, 74-75
     balancing, 62-63
     maintaining, 74-75
     testing, 63
  Waterfalls, 37-50
     flexible liners, 43, 46-48
     planning, 38
     preformed, 43-45
     pumps for, 38-41
     streams with, 42
     types, 41
  Weir, 39, 41
  Wind, effect on pond, 6-7
  Windbreaks, 7
  Wiring, 9, 49
  Wood edgings, 13
  Wooden bridges, 58-59
- Zoning ordinances, 22